GET
MOTIVATED!

GET MOTIVATED!

OVERCOME ANY OBSTACLE,
ACHIEVE ANY GOAL,
AND ACCELERATE YOUR SUCCESS
WITH MOTIVATIONAL DNA™

Tamara Lowe

DOUBLEDAY
New York   London   Toronto   Sydney   Auckland

DD

DOUBLEDAY

Copyright © 2009 by Tamara Lowe

All Rights Reserved
Published in the United States by Doubleday,
an imprint of The Doubleday Publishing Group,
a division of Random House, Inc., New York.
www.doubleday.com

Doubleday is a registered trademark and the DD colophon
is a trademark of Random House, Inc.
All trademarks are the property of their respective companies.

Book design by Chris Welch
Cataloging-in-Publication Data is on file with the Library of Congress

ISBN 978-0-385-52469-8
PRINTED IN THE UNITED STATES OF AMERICA
3   5   7   9   10   8   6   4   2

Dedicated to the three men in my life:

MY MOTIVATION
Peter, you are my very best friend,
my hero, and my one true love.

MY INSPIRATION
Zack, you challenge me, make me laugh,
and inspire me like no one else ever has.

MY CELEBRATION
Blaize, you are my joy, my delight,
and the kiss of Heaven in my life.

CONTENTS

Fulfillment • Eight Ways to Win in Your Relationships • The Five Pillars of Perfect Health • FREE BONUS #16: *"Living a Life of Purpose"* podcast by Tamara Lowe, plus *"Steps to Discovering Your Spiritual Purpose,"* a 15-page Special Report

FOREWORD BY RUDY GIULIANI

In nearly forty years of public life, I have had the opportunity to work with many of the world's greatest leaders in business, justice, entertainment, academia, philanthropy, and yes, government. Their personalities, perspectives, and political views differ, but one thing all great leaders have in common is a powerful motivation to succeed. These people are not necessarily more brilliant or talented than others—but their drive to succeed causes them to get up earlier, stay up later, and try harder than their sometimes more gifted peers. To borrow a page from Ecclesiastes, "The race is not to the swift, nor the battle to the strong, nor bread to the wise, nor riches to the intelligent, nor favor to the men of skill." In my observation, success and significance in life belong to the motivated.

When I was growing up, my parents and teachers motivated me to live a life of integrity, to serve others, and to act with courage—even in the most difficult of times. As U.S. Attorney, Mayor, and now in my business and law practice, I am constantly on the lookout for motivated people. I like to hire them, I like to promote them, and I like to empower them so that they can transform the world around them, Motivated people take action. They turn dreaming into doing. In fact, motivation is at the very heart of achievement, change, and success.

That is why I am so pleased to write this foreword for my good friend Tamara Lowe. If there is anyone who is qualified to write about motivation, it's Tamara Lowe. No one else in the history of business seminars has motivated as many through live events. Tamara Lowe gathers the world's greatest achievers and persuades them to set aside their busy schedules in order to share their insights with the business and community leaders who attend her events. This facilitates a transfer of intellectual wealth that energizes our businesses, stimulates our economy, and empowers people to succeed. Tamara, along with her husband, Peter, and their wonderful team, has produced these dynamic forums in every major city in America, over and over again, for more than two decades.

When I learned how to play golf, a friend told me, "Don't worry about the score. Hit what you can. Advance the ball. Just improve yourself." Without question, the best way to improve yourself is with training. So I took lessons, I bought a few videotapes, I practiced, and my game improved dramatically. As you master the strategies that Tamara Lowe presents in *Get Motivated!* your ability to motivate yourself and others will improve substantially. This is important when things are going well in life, but it is crucial during times of crisis. That's when training and preparation really pay off.

One of the first things that I did when I became Mayor of New York City was to start a new agency, the Office of Emergency Management. We pulled together the emergency response for the police department, the fire department, all of the public health agencies, and the emergency services divisions. The agency was designed to coordinate emergency efforts, and we staged drills and tabletop exercises for a wide variety of scenarios, including a sarin gas attack, plane crashes, anthrax, and suicide bombings.

On September 11, 2001, no one had prepared for the notion that planes full of ordinary citizens would be hijacked and turned into missiles aimed at our most-populated buildings. Because we had prepared for every emergency we could imagine, we were far better prepared for one that no one had imagined. We had trained for exactly the kind of multi-dimensional, large-scale attack that was perpetrated on New York City. I believe our response to the attack showed a readiness that not only saved thousands of lives but actually helped start the process of showing the rest of America and the world that our spirit would not be broken.

The value of preparation cannot be overstated. The expert training that Tamara Lowe provides will help you bring out the best in yourself, your family, friends, co-workers, and clients—in good times and in challenging times. There are two key components to achievement: extensive information and appropriate action. For example, when I became Mayor of New York, crime in our city was out of control. We gathered extensive information by looking at crime statistics neighborhood by neighborhood. If we spotted an increase in crime, we took immediate action, increasing the number of police officers in that area or modifying our tactics to snuff out the problem before it grew. This achieved a favorable result and the crime rate declined so rapidly that New York City went from being the nation's crime capital to being the safest large city in America.

I have discovered that my success hinges on motivating those around me to achieve their best, to excel at levels that surpass what they even thought possible. The genius of Tamara Lowe's Motivational DNA model is its simplicity: Is a person driven to compete or cooperate? Do they need stability or variety? Do they desire internal awards or external?

With this basic framework in place, it's possible to read people fast. And with this knowledge, you can inspire others to perform at their apex. I encourage you to read this groundbreaking book and implement the principles that Tamara Lowe teaches. You will not be disappointed. In fact, you'll be inspired, just as I was.

Rudy Giuliani
New York
October 2008

PREFACE BY PETER LOWE

My business partner, Tamara Lowe, for more than twenty-one years has also been the love of my life and the wife of my dreams. I'm certain that any positive words I might offer about this book may be seen as biased. Still, I'd like to say a few words to you, the reader.

No one else truly knows you the way your own spouse does. So I'd like to give you an insider's perspective from someone who has been happily married to the author of *Get Motivated!* for over two decades. It is said in jest, "You are your own worst critic . . . unless you're married!" Thankfully, my wife has found nothing but good in me and has always been my biggest supporter and cheerleader. But I'd like to tell you something about her. Something that I feel you, the reader of this book, deserve to know . . .

I have always been saddened when women attendees of our seminars tell me that they have been successful in business, but that they feel they've failed in their relationships. There is a certain expectation that our culture imposes on them, and that women place upon themselves, to be "Superwoman." So many women have told me that they feel it's an impossible ideal and that they struggle to balance career and family. And yes, it's true that men struggle with a similar balancing act. Allow me to speak a word of encouragement to you: It's not impossible. You really can find a happy balance in your life, and my best advice to you would be to consider Tamara's example.

This is a woman who possesses not only a brilliant mind for business, but also godly wisdom, sincere love for others and a mother's heart. She has devoted herself to me and our children while working tirelessly in our company, traveling, and speaking—and has still managed to find time for volunteerism, exercise, cooking, helping with homework, and the endless other demands of life. The fruit of Tamara's balanced approach to life is seen in our marriage. It is evident in our children. And it can be seen in the countless lives she has touched. If ever there were an individual to model for success in life, it is the woman that I have the great privilege to call my very best friend and wife, Tamara Lowe.

ACKNOWLEDGMENTS

I gave my first motivational speech at the age of four. It is one of my earliest memories. The room was packed with several hundred salespeople at a network marketing conference. I don't know if I was a good speaker or merely a little novelty, but I do remember the standing ovation. I've been in love with the audience ever since.

Thank you, Mom and Dad, for discovering early on that I had no fear of public speaking. Thank you for putting me onstage at a young age and nudging me toward my destiny. I am forever grateful for your love, encouragement, care, concern, and friendship. You are truly wonderful!

It is impossible to express adequate appreciation for Peter, Zack, and Blaize Lowe, to whom this book is dedicated, and without whom it would not have been possible. You are the loves of my life. Thank you for the sacrifices you've made. My life is complete because of you.

I also want to say thank you to Eric and Margie Lowe, my precious in-laws. I would have married Peter just to get you!

This book, like every other significant accomplishment in my life, is the result of a huge team effort. I am deeply indebted to the following people, to whom I extend my sincerest gratitude and thanks:

Bonnie Solow, my incredibly gifted literary agent and friend. You are everything I hoped for in an agent and much, much more. Thank you for your wisdom, guidance, dedication, sensitivity, gutsiness, and integrity. Words cannot convey how much I appreciate and admire you.

Michael Palgon, the deputy publisher of Random House. Thank you for your vision for this book, your support for me as a first-time author, and for conveying your excitement about the book to the whole Random House team.

Roger Scholl, my fantastic editor at Doubleday. I am so thankful for the enormous amount of time and energy you put into this book, and for guiding me in these uncharted waters of publishing. Thanks for laboring with me over the manuscript and joining me in my obsession to give the readers our very best work.

Liz Hazelton, Julie Sills, Orli Moscowitz, Anna Thompson, and the entire energetic, creative, supportive team at Random House. I extend my sincere appreciation for your enthusiasm and hard work. You have been a delight to work with.

Rich Taylor, Jean Traina, Doug Scaletta, Katie Meehan, Kim Davidson, and Shelly Ballestero, who were responsible for the terrific cover of *Get Motivated!* Thank you with all my heart!

Chris Fortunato, who did such a wonderful job of overseeing the copyediting and typesetting of the book.

Jenny Meyer, our awesome foreign rights agent. Thank you for taking *Get Motivated!* to the ends of the earth.

Brian Forte, the senior vice president of GET MOTIVATED Seminars and one of my champions. Your love, loyalty, friendship, encouragement, competence, creativity, and hilarious wit have made it a pure joy to work with you. You inspire me. What are the chances that I'd have a genius for a brother?

Rick Nash, my brilliant director of strategic research. Your wholehearted support has meant the world to me. I cannot begin to articulate my gratitude for your wise counsel, my appreciation for your generous spirit, or my esteem for your great intellect.

My highly motivated research and support team: Alison Kilmartin, Kevin Lyons, Sydney Trinh, Matt Mallette, Younes Sikel, Daniel Ajo, Brad DeRosia, Brad Atchison, Shanelle Francis, Summer Wright, Hannah Newlin, Stephanie Lederle, Suzie Barbour, Alesya Izoita, Mary Kate Smith, Lauren Lett, Linda Becker, and Mandi Rivieccio. This book would not have been possible without your tireless and invaluable assistance. Thank you for accomplishing my many impossible requests, and doing it with enviable excellence.

Faith Catherman, Dida Cuevas, Dan Miller, Lucia Gonzales, and Eric Ensign, who gave me the home court advantage. Endless thanks for taking care of me and my family when my head was in the book.

Eddie and Alice Smith and every member of the "Prayer Force." Thank you for having my back!

Ida, Ricardo, and Andres Leguizamon, true friends whom I adore. You've opened doors of opportunity to me and challenged me to step through them with boldness.

Amy Jones and Keith Craft, for pinch-hitting for me on numerous occasions.

Lance and Annabelle Wallnau, Bob and Laura Larson, and Bill and Linda McGrane, my dear friends. Thank you for sharing your brilliance, expertise, and exhaustive vocabulary.

Lynton and Judy Turkington, for inspiring me with your authenticity. You are the real deal!

My beloved friends and mentors: Charles and Barbara Green,

Andrew Lloyd, David and Ina Newell, Dave and Kathy Gales, Tom and Donna Mullins, Paul and Claire Hollis, Gene and Terri Bacon, Norman and Judy Benz, Rich and Lindsey Larson, and Steve and Gill Barry. Thank you for pushing me beyond my comfort zone.

My author and speaker friends who advised, encouraged, and inspired me: John Maxwell, Suze Orman, Kathy Travis, Pat Williams, Brian Tracy, Linda Brook, John Perkins, Julie Norman, Michael Pink, Phil Town, Jordan Rubin, Robert Schuller, and Zig Ziglar. Thank you for your encouragement and insightful advice and for answering my never-ending questions.

To the many family members and friends who cheered me on, I am so deeply moved by your love and support. Your excitement about this book buoyed me. Thank you, dear ones!

Finally, to the millions of people who have attended our events, and to our sensational team at GET MOTIVATED Seminars who make it all possible, I cannot thank you enough. You have been such an integral part of my life and have enriched it beyond measure.

PART ONE

THE NEW SCIENCE OF SUCCESS

The Four Laws of Motivation

If someone had told me twenty-eight years ago—when I was a drug addict and dealer—that I would soon be working with U.S. Presidents and world leaders, I would have thought they were smoking the same stuff I was smoking!

I grew up on the streets of New Orleans, a party town where Mardi Gras never ends. I started using drugs at the age of ten. By twelve I was dealing. I dropped out of school not long after that. I never made it past the eighth grade. What happened next is a blur. There is a whole decade of my life that I don't remember very well. I went from one high to the next, barely coming up for air. Then I had an amazing, life-transforming experience that changed me forever, and *I got motivated!* Powerful strategies were revealed to me that I am going to share with you throughout this book.

I got off drugs, earned a high school equivalency diploma, and went to college. I planned to spend the rest of my life helping the people I understood best: addicts, alcoholics, the homeless, the poor, and the abused. Instead, in one of the most stunning surprises of my life, I found myself working with business leaders, professional athletes, politicians, heads of state, music superstars, Hollywood celebrities, and the most influential people of our time.

The day the Secret Service ushered me into a limo with President Ronald Reagan (the first of five U.S. Presidents that I have been honored to serve), it hit home for me just how radically my life had changed. As a consultant, personal coach, and entrepreneur, I am now in the position to help motivate scores of people—from Olympic gold medalists and corporate executives to middle managers and college students. The company that my husband and I started produces the world's largest business seminars. Through our GET MOTIVATED Business Seminars we've taught more than two million people how to advance in their careers, improve their relationships, make more money, achieve their goals, and experience greater fulfillment in their personal lives.

Literally tens of thousands of people pack the biggest sports arenas in America for our GET MOTIVATED Business Seminars. I host about thirty of these events every year—in Miami, Chicago, Los Angeles, Atlanta, Seattle, Dallas, Denver, and every other major U.S. city from coast to coast.

The *Washington Post* describes our seminars as "the Super Bowl of Success." The *New York Times* says we "rouse sales reps, entrepreneurs and executives to higher levels of business performance." *Time* magazine calls us "the motivational Dream Team." And the *Wall Street Journal* raves that our events are "a barnstorming feel-good tour de force." Honestly, it blows my mind when I hear these kinds of accolades. I'm a former drug dealer and dropout. People with my background normally don't live to tell the tale let alone have an opportunity to experience life at this level. I am incredibly humbled by it all.

Why Successful People Succeed

This book is about motivation—how you can motivate yourself and others, quickly and easily. The system I am about to unveil is based on an eight-year study that my team and I have conducted with more than 10,000 people.[1] It is a research-based, systematic approach to achievement—and it works.

I've spent the past twenty-five years of my life with some of the greatest achievers on earth. They all have different talents, personalities, and skills. But they have one thing in common: Each of them is *highly motivated*. In fact, the more motivated a person is, the more success he or she experiences. Motivated people advance farther and faster in their careers, earn more money, are more productive, experience more satisfying relationships, and are happier than the less motivated people around them.

In fact, I'll go so far as to say that *motivation is one of the greatest keys to success* in every area of our lives. Education is important, but motivation is more important. Talent counts, but motivation counts more. Your network of contacts is valuable, but your personal motivation trumps all of these things.

Would you like to have more passion and energy to achieve your goals? When you feel your motivation fading, would you like to know how to instantly reignite it? Wouldn't it be great to have the ability to motivate the people you love—your spouse, children, friends, and family—and help them to excel? Do you want to know the secrets of inspiring your coworkers and colleagues to perform like champions? I have good news for you. Exciting new research has now shown us exactly how to *activate and sustain motivation*—and that's what this book is all about.

Motivation is the power that creates action. It's like the gas in your car that makes it go. You could have a Bugatti Veyron, a million-dollar marvel of automotive technology, but without gas, that car won't take you anywhere. The same is true of motivation; *it is the fuel of success*. A person could have all the intelligence, talent, and opportunity in the world—but without motivation, all that potential will go nowhere.

Most of us have not been as successful as we would like—and I believe there is a reason for that. We simply didn't know how to harness the power of motivation. After all, motivation is difficult to understand. One day we feel motivated . . . and then the next day we don't. We can be fired up in the morning but burned out by lunchtime. When we feel motivated, we're not always sure *why*. Even worse, we never know how long our motivation will last. And when we are unmotivated, we usually have no idea how to stir up energy and excitement. Motivation is unpredictable. It seems to come and go, as random and fleeting as the wind.

The mystery of motivation has puzzled educators, employers, and behavioral scientists for centuries. How can managers inspire their employees and their teams to be more productive? What is the best way for parents to motivate their children? How can teachers engage disinterested students? How can coaches provoke their athletes to excel and win championships? Perhaps most important of all, what can each of us do to motivate ourselves?

Until now motivation has been a hit-or-miss game, like throwing darts blindfolded and hoping one will strike the target. Sometimes we accidentally hit upon a strategy that works, but more often than not we miss the mark. This awkward, haphazard approach to motivation fails to produce dependable results. You may think, *There's got to be a better way*. I'm here to tell you that there is.

Within the pages of this book, you will receive the tools and technology to crack the code of motivation. I'm going to show you a quick, easy, reliable way to motivate yourself and others for maximum achievement. You will not only learn how to *get motivated*, you'll also find out how to *stay motivated*.

Whether you are a manager looking to motivate your team, or an individual seeking to realize your personal goals, *Get Motivated* can help. Do you want to increase your income, stop smoking, start your own business, lose weight, or improve your health? I'm going to show you how to generate the motivation needed to do all those things and more. Are you a parent or teacher who wants to learn the secrets of motivating children? This book will show you exactly how to do that. In fact, *Get Motivated* can help you improve and enrich all of your relationships.

You are going to learn how to profile the Motivational DNA of others so that, in just a few seconds, you will know exactly what makes them tick, how to best communicate with them, connect with them, inspire and motivate them. And you'll learn precisely how to motivate yourself as well.

MOTIVATION IS NOT ONE-SIZE-FITS-ALL

Most motivational books offer little more than recycled platitudes and simplistic solutions. They are the literary equivalent of Kool-Aid. Sugar without substance. They all seem to follow the same format, promising "Ten Simple Steps to Achieving Your Dreams." The simple steps are so simple, in fact, that we already know what they are. Work smarter, not harder. . . . Have a good attitude. . . . Set goals. . . . Think positive. . . . Never give up. . . . And so on. If that's what you were expecting from this book, let me assure you that I am not going to bore you into a cliché-induced coma. The insights and methodology that I am about to show you offer a fresh and practical approach to motivation. I will not insult your intelligence by serving up a big bowl of motivational mush. I promise not to feed you any monotone maxims, dim-witted hype, predictable proverbs, or pabulum. This book is for grown-ups.

The fact of the matter is that everyone cannot follow the same "ten simple steps" and get the same result. It is statistically improbable that even *ten* people following the same steps can get the same result. Motivation is a uniquely individual force.

In the same way that each person has a different fingerprint and a distinctive combination of DNA, every individual is hardwired with a specific motivational pattern. What motivates me is probably not going to motivate you. And if I attempt to motivate you using strategies that work for me, the likelihood of its succeeding is exceedingly slim. In order to effectively motivate yourself and others, you must first understand the Four Laws of Motivation.

LAW #1: EVERYONE IS MOTIVATED DIFFERENTLY

I have studied the dynamics of human achievement for more than two decades. After evaluating the data, I am convinced of what Zig Ziglar has said from our platform many times; there are no "unmotivated" people. That may surprise you, but it's true. Everyone is motivated. Even crooks and criminals are motivated. Bank robbers are motivated to rob banks and drug addicts are motivated to do drugs. They are motivated, but by the wrong things. Nevertheless, it is possible for everyone to be motivated properly—and this is the secret to high-level achievement.

Although everyone is motivated, we are all motivated *differently*. That is why you'll sometimes hear parents say, "After my first child, I thought I had parenting figured out. Then my second child came along and all the rules changed!" What worked well with the first child may not work at all with the second. You see, even in childhood we each have our own unique motivational code.

Why do you suppose managers have such a difficult time energizing departments or igniting team morale? It is because every single team member is motivated differently. Managers usually try to increase productivity by using strategies that they themselves find motivational. When those tactics aren't effective with some of their employees, the managers conclude, "These employees are unmotivated." That's a terrible mistake. Most employees are *very motivated*. But they may not be motivated by the same drivers that motivate their manager.

LAW #2: EACH INDIVIDUAL HAS A UNIQUE AND DISTINCT MOTIVATIONAL TYPE

Every person has *a unique achievement pattern*, or what I call Motivational DNA.

Just as your genetic DNA determines your physical attributes, Motivational DNA dictates how you are best motivated. Your Motivational DNA is composed of the "drives," "needs," and "awards" that motivate you.

Your motivational *Drives, Needs,* and *Awards,* or DNA, combine to form a pattern that is every bit as unique as your fingerprint. Metaphorically speaking, these factors are encoded in you at conception and remain the same throughout your life. It's not something you can change or alter. It is a part of who you are.

Every one of us is hardwired with a precise motivational matrix that determines exactly what motivates us and what doesn't. What works for someone else may not work for you. Why? It's in the DNA. You were made to be motivated in a specific way. There are certain motivators that excite and inspire you, and other motivators that you dislike and don't work.

Here's why this is fundamentally important: *The quality of your life is largely determined by your motivation.* The successes or failures of your relationships, finances, health, personal goals, and professional endeavors are all shaped by Motivational DNA. Not only that, your ability to energize and motivate those around you is directly connected to your skill in decoding their motivational types.

Exceptional leaders intuitively recognize and respond to the motivational styles of those around them. They instinctively sense how to inspire themselves and others. What has been absent is a usable methodology for the rest of us. Motivational DNA provides that missing link.

Cracking the Motivational Code

I first began to develop the Motivational DNA research that I will outline in this book in 1999. Since then, clients, counselors, and educators around the world have participated in the process. My team and I have conducted primary research with more than 10,000 people in virtually every field of occupation: business, medicine, education, government, the arts, entertainment, sports, science, law, and finance.

The quest to unravel what motivates people has taken me to more than seventy countries. I've conferred with kings, prime ministers, and presidents. I have personally interviewed virtually every winning Super Bowl coach and quarterback of the past two decades. I've worked with Academy Award–winning actors, Grammy Award–winning musicians, Olympians, *New York Times* bestselling authors, NBA all-stars, baseball Hall of Famers, millionaires, billionaires, and A-list celebrities— a Who's Who of success. This helped me to identify the similarities, trends, behaviors, and qualities that motivate people to achieve outstanding results.

Many times I was mystified by the seemingly arbitrary nature of success. How could one person with extraordinary talent, passion, and commitment succeed, while someone else with an equal amount of talent, passion, and commitment fail? I was often left with more questions than answers.

- Is motivation internal or external? Environmental or genetic?
- Can motivation alone change undesirable behaviors?
- Are motivated people born or made?
- Is it possible to motivate someone to do something they truly don't want to do?
- What types of incentives motivate people best?

This last question was the real catalyst for my breakthrough. After years of research, my team and I found that there are eighty-one specific things that people say motivate them—everything from love to money, from curiosity to contribution, from feeling valued to the fear of failure. By reducing these motivators to their most fundamental form, we discovered six factors that actually encompass all eighty-one motivators. By decoding the precise combination of these elements, you can unlock a person's ability to succeed at the highest levels.

My team and I discovered a pattern that correlated consistently across a broad spectrum of people, regardless of age, gender, personality, race, religion, or education. In short, our findings on Motivational DNA really worked! And it worked the same way for everyone, male and female, old and young.

LAW #3: WHAT MOTIVATES ONE PERSON CAN DE-MOTIVATE ANOTHER

I first stumbled upon Motivational DNA with two children: my sons, Zack and Blaize. At the time, the boys were five and ten years old. Although they had the same parents, lived in the same home, attended the same school and church, and were involved in the same sports, the brothers were polar opposites in terms of temperament. While both of them were intelligent, attractive, and athletic, their dispositions were complete contrasts. The younger one was cheerful, cooperative, outgoing, and good-natured. Our older child was sullen, contrary, introverted, and pessimistic. Both were terrific kids, but the younger one was always more motivated and enthusiastic.

Unfortunately, I made a common mistake—one that is inevitable until you understand the nature of Motivational DNA. I assumed that I had one motivated child and one child who was less motivated. What I didn't realize at the time was that I actually had *two* highly motivated children. However, I was motivating one of them correctly and the other one incorrectly. In fact, I was so unskilled at motivating my older son, Zack, that I was actually *de-motivating* him. I was using the same motivational strategies with Zack that I applied with his younger brother, Blaize. But because the motivational types of these two children are on opposite sides of the spectrum, the motivators that worked so well with Blaize made matters worse with Zack.

As I now know, Zack's motivational type is what I call a PSE. In the terminology of Motivational DNA, that means he has a Production Drive, a Need for Stability, and is validated by External Awards. (I'll explain these concepts in more detail shortly.) Blaize, on the other hand, is a CVI motivational type. He has a Connection Drive, a Variety Need, and is validated by Internal Awards. For now all you need to know is that these two children have no overlapping motivational factors. They require completely different strategies to motivate them.

As a mother, I was frustrated with the situation at home. Zack required so much attention that I felt Blaize (the one I thought was more cooperative and motivated) was being shortchanged. It seemed unfair that most of my parenting time was spent correcting, cajoling, and scolding Zack, while Blaize's reward for good behavior was to be overlooked.

This is ridiculous! I thought. *I'm a motivational speaker and educator—I should be able to motivate my own ten-year-old son!* Zack seemed to be a square peg in the round hole of our family circle, and I couldn't figure out why. Blaize was an animated, expressive, confident child. Zack barely spoke above a whisper in public. Blaize could carry on a lively twenty-minute conversation with any adult he met, while Zack couldn't even look a grown-up in the eye when he shook hands. The rest of our family are "glass-is-half-full" optimists, while all Zack could see was the black cloud that dwarfed every silver lining.

The interesting thing to me was that Zack had been this way all his life. The first conversation I had with Zack occurred when he was fourteen months old and had scarcely a dozen words in his vocabulary. Zack was whining and crying at the time. He was in a foul mood and I was trying to figure out how to console him.

I said, "Zack, do you want a bottle?"

"NO!" he shouted.

"Are you hungry?" I asked.

"NO!"

"Are you tired? Do you want to lie down?"

"NO! NO!"

"Why don't we watch *Sesame Street* together?"

"NO!"

"Would you like to play with your toys or go to the park?"

"NO!"

And so it went.

Exasperated, I finally said, "Is NO the only word that you can say?"

He lifted his chubby little leg and stomped his foot on the ground. "NO!" he yelled. "NO WAY!"

What I did not understand at the time—or even a full decade later—was that Zack was hardwired with a particular Motivational DNA. In an effort to understand my child, I administered some of the testing methods that I use to help my coaching clients. We did personality tests, strength assessments, listening exercises, and numerous other evaluations. It was through this process that I stumbled upon the hidden achievement code of Motivational DNA and began to unravel its secrets.

Applying the techniques outlined in this book, I saw instantaneous changes in Zack. The changes took place so quickly, it was shocking. That's when I knew I was on to something. I began to motivate Zack using incentives that were compatible with his motivational type, and he blossomed. He went from being uncooperative and contrary to cooperative and agreeable. The child who previously complained about every chore was suddenly cleaning his room without being asked and offering to take out the trash. Two months later, the shy, introverted boy who could not raise his voice above a whisper in public auditioned for the school play and landed the leading role. In fact, the more that my husband and I used the techniques I am going to show you, the more motivated Zack became.

In the three years since then, Zack has become one of the most popular and outgoing kids at his school. His grade point average has skyrocketed from 2.8 to 3.9. Zack is now a star player on his football team and excels at everything he tries. In fact, his teachers and classmates voted him "Most Motivational Leader" at school. Zack was also selected from several thousand adolescents as one of just fourteen delegates to attend an elite youth leadership-training program.

Last summer, Zack helped me emcee several of our GET MOTIVATED Seminars and spoke like a pro before audiences of more than 18,000 people. He even conducted onstage interviews with several NFL stars using a Q&A format—*without cue cards!* His professionalism, poise, and witty comebacks were so impressive that after the athletes left the stage, the audience gave Zack a standing ovation. This is an example of the power of Motivational DNA—it works.

LAW #4: NO ONE MOTIVATIONAL TYPE IS "BETTER" THAN ANY OTHER

Remember, everyone is motivated differently and that's okay. There is no "best" Motivational DNA, just as there is no "best" blood type. You may have Type A while I have Type B, but neither blood type is better than the other. They are equally good—until one of us needs a blood transfusion; then it is crucial to have a donor with a compatible type. Giving someone the wrong type of blood can be fatal.

In the same way, if I try to motivate someone using strategies that are effective for my motivational profile, it can absolutely *kill* the other person's motivation. Strategies that work amazingly well for your Motivational DNA can actually be *de-motivating* for someone who has a different motivational type.

Let me give you an example to describe this. I have a keyless electronic safe in my home. The safe has a digital keypad that is programmed to unlock the vault when I press a six-digit code in a specific sequence. When I press the right numbers in the correct sequence, the door opens. If I press the wrong numbers, a fast beeping noise indicates that

I entered an incorrect code and I need to try again. If I do not input the correct code within three tries, the system will shut down. Then the safe will not accept any more codes—even the correct code. Sadly, a similar process takes place with people. If you keep attempting to motivate them in the wrong way, they shut down. They lock up. This is why it is essential to understand, decipher, and apply the code-cracking skills of Motivational DNA.

Motivational DNA may sound complex, but it is actually quite easy to understand. In this book, I will teach you everything you need to know to use this process successfully.

Just as biological DNA is composed of individual genes that are linked together, Motivational DNA consists of specific factors that are linked together.

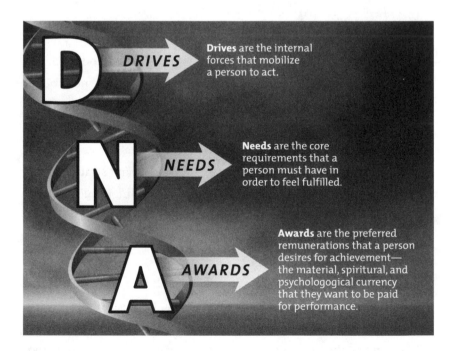

Drives are the internal forces that mobilize a person to act.

Needs are the core requirements that a person must have in order to feel fulfilled.

Awards are the preferred remunerations that a person desires for achievement—the material, spiritual, and psychological currency that they want to be paid for performance.

Motivational DNA is made up of Drives, Needs, and Awards:

- The Drives for *connection* and/or *production* are the internal forces that mobilize a person to act.
- The Needs for *stability* and/or *variety* are core requirements that a person must have in order to feel fulfilled.
- *Internal* and/or *External* Awards are the types of compensation or remuneration a person desires to reward achievement and encourage performance.

I have organized the six elements of Motivational DNA below in an easy-to-follow chart.

D DRIVES	**N** NEEDS	**A** AWARDS
Connection	Stability	Internal
Production	Variety	External

All six of these motivators (Connection, Production, Stability, Variety, Internal Awards, and External Awards) inspire everyone. To one degree or another, all of us desire Connection with other people and we all like to be Productive. Everyone wants to experience some measure of both Stability and Variety. We all crave Internal Awards (like appreciation) as well as External Awards (like financial compensation). However, each of us has a definite preference for *three of these motivators*.

THE THREE-QUESTION TEST

I have asked thousands of people the following three questions. They are simple indicators of deeply ingrained achievement patterns. To get a quick reading of your own Motivational DNA, ask yourself the three questions below. This will give you a simple assessment of your basic motivational makeup.

1. **Do you tend to be more competitive or cooperative?**

   Competitive people have what I call a Production Drive. They are inclined to be task-oriented. Cooperative people, on the other hand, have what I term a Connection Drive—in other words, they tend to be people-oriented or people-centric.

2. **Do you prefer constancy or change?**

   People who prefer constancy have what I refer to as a Stability Need—a desire for consistency, order, and routine. In contrast, people who prefer change have what I call a Variety Need. They are stimulated by new experiences and energized by change.

3. **Which would make you feel more valued at work: sincere *appreciation* without a financial bonus, or a *bonus* without appreciation?**

   If you'd rather have appreciation, you possess what I call an Internal Award system—one characterized by private recognition and contribution. If you'd rather have the monetary bonus, you have what I call an External Award system—one characterized by public recognition and opportunity for advancement.

This three-question survey offers a fast and simple way to determine your motivational type. When you take the twenty-one-question profile in Chapter 2, I'll help you drill down deeper to find your primary Motivational DNA. You'll also learn how to motivate yourself according to your type.

Keep in mind that your achievement patterns can differ in various settings or in different contexts. What motivates you in one setting may shift, depending on whether you are at home, at work, with friends, or in a learning environment. For example, my husband, Peter, has an off-the-charts Production Drive at work, as he races to accomplish challenging goals. At home, however, his primary drive shifts to Connection, as he balances his Production Drive with his need for supportive personal relationships that are separate and distinct from his professional obligations.

In the same way that the facets of a diamond refract different prisms of color depending on how the light hits it, so each of us reflects a variety of motivational tendencies in different aspects of our lives. At work, you may have a strong need for Stability as you methodically prioritize and execute tasks, but in your personal relationships your primary need may shift to one of Variety as you seek to have fun, learn, travel, and grow with those you love.

As you get older, or as the priorities of your life change, your motivational preferences may also vary. Just as physical changes occur as we age (even though our genetic DNA remains the same), our motivational preferences may alter as we get older (even though our basic motivational makeup remains the same). The better you understand the basic principles and dynamics of Motivational DNA, the easier it will be to motivate yourself, and others, in various settings.

THE FOUR LAWS OF MOTIVATION

1

Everyone is motivated—but each of us is motivated *differently*.

2

Each individual is created from conception with a unique and
distinct motivational type.

3

The very things that inspire and excite one motivational type may
cause another to disengage. What motivates one type can
de-motivate another.

4

No one motivational type is "better" than any other.

MOTIVATION LEAVES CLUES

When I was eight years old, my parents took me to a country fair. At
one booth, local policemen were fingerprinting children. A tall, friendly
police officer pressed my thumb on a black pad and then onto a little
card. While I examined my ink-stained thumb, he looked at my fingerprint. The policeman grinned slowly, handed me the card, and said,
"You were a thumb sucker, weren't you?"

I was a little embarrassed and more than a little surprised. How
could he tell that by looking at my thumbprint?

The policeman pointed to a little dent on my thumb, which I still have to this day. He said, "Kids who suck their thumb get a dip that shows up on their fingerprints."

He could tell something about me that other people didn't know—and something that I didn't want to reveal—just by glancing at a few distinguishing characteristics. The same is true of Motivational DNA. When you master this methodology, you will know how to motivate yourself and others by zeroing in on a few recognizable signs. It even works when the people you wish to motivate don't want to reveal (or simply don't know) what motivates them.

Now let's examine the six factors of Motivational DNA under a microscope, as it were, to see what they look like and how they differ.

Drives: The Internal Forces That Mobilize a Person to Act

PRODUCTION DRIVE

Individuals with a Production Drive tend to focus on achievement and value results. Producers are usually strategic thinkers and problem solvers. They exhibit strong leadership potential and are able to thrive under pressure. Those who have a Production Drive are typically persistent, energetic, and confident. They are able to organize people and move projects forward. Bill Gates, Barbara Walters, and Lance Armstrong are all examples of Producers.

CONNECTION DRIVE

Individuals with a Connection Drive move toward affiliation and value relationships. Connectors are usually friendly, reliable, and well liked by others. They are empathetic listeners who provide the speaker with a sounding board. Those with a Connection Drive are supportive, loyal, inclusive, and collaborative. They promote teamwork, harmony, and community. They are the kind of individuals who celebrate the success of others.

Every motivational type can exhibit less favorable qualities as well. I think of these negative elements as "mutant strains." In biology, mutation occurs when there is a sudden structural change in the DNA. When mutation occurs, properties or traits not found in the original DNA are created. A mutant strain can result in genetic disorders or other nonbeneficial characteristics, such as spina bifida or Down syndrome. Similarly, "mutant strains" in our motivational DNA can produce disruptive behaviors.

For example, because of their intense focus on achieving results, **Producers** can be overly competitive, exhibiting the kind of win-at-all-costs behavior that may upset friends and colleagues. **Connectors**, on the other hand, can be too pliable and accommodating. They may allow others to take advantage of them or go out of their way to avoid healthy conflict.

Needs: The Core Requirements That a Person Must Have in Order to Feel Fulfilled

THE NEED FOR STABILITY

People who have a Stability Need enjoy routines. They are good with schedules, systems, and organization. They are usually practical, methodical, and responsible. Stabilizers like to follow procedure and obey the rules. They find comfort in the predictable. They value accuracy and are logical (rather than emotional) in their decision making. Those with a Stability Need tend to be careful and consistent. They are great operations people; they are the sort of people who make the trains run on time. Stabilizers refine ideas and improve processes.

THE NEED FOR VARIETY

People who have what I call a Variety Need enjoy change. They tend to be animated, persuasive, and spontaneous. Variables are not flustered by rapid transitions or last-minute modifications. They have an ability to shift gears and turn on a dime. They are confident in their ability to master new skills. Variables are usually fun-loving and enthusiastic. They typically have a hunger for adventure and crave new experiences.

There are also possible downsides, or mutant strains, of Stabilizers and Variables:

- **Stabilizers** at times can experience paralysis by analysis. They can be too slow to take action because they feel they need more time to analyze the options or lack enough data to make a good decision. They may also become inflexible to change and resist innovation. Stabilizers are often the ones who play devil's advocate to new ideas or projects.
- **Variables**, on the other hand, have a tendency to underanalyze risks. They may become so excited about a new idea or direction that they dive in the water without measuring its depth. They may grow intolerant of routine and want rapid change in spite of potential consequences. While Stabilizers may think without acting, Variables can act without thinking.

Awards: How a Person Desires to Be Compensated for Achievement—The Material, Spiritual, and Psychological Currency a Person Wants to Be Paid for Performance

INTERNAL AWARDS

Individuals who have an Internal Award system feel validated and esteemed by sincere appreciation. They are "mission-minded" people with a need to make a positive difference. They value contribution. Internals generally prefer private recognition to public recognition. They derive satisfaction from meaningful work. Psychological pay is of primary importance to them. They need to feel good about what they are doing. Internals are motivated by a good working environment, coworkers they like, the opportunity for personal growth, and receiving specific positive feedback.

EXTERNAL AWARDS

Individuals with an External Award system feel validated by tangible benefits. They value hard work and believe that winning should be rewarded. Externals enjoy public recognition by their superiors, special privileges, and freedom from controls. Fair pay is of primary importance to them. They need to be compensated financially in a way that is commensurate with their labor. Externals are motivated by salary, bonuses, authority, opportunity to advance, private offices, and perks.

Regrettably, our culture tends to regard those with an Internal Award system as virtuous, whereas those with an External Award system are perceived as greedy. While Internals are seen as selfless, Externals are classified as selfish. But that kind of stereotyping is devaluing and destructive—and untrue. My brother Brian happens to be an External. He is motivated by money. He is also one of the most generous people I've ever known. He donates liberally to countless organizations and children's charities. Nobody who knows my brother would think of him as greedy. To the contrary, he is an extremely kindhearted and giving man who happens to be motivated by an External Award system. Awards are not a measure of character; they are simply factors that make a person feel esteemed and appreciated. Remember, there are no "best" types, only different types.

Living in the Achievement Zone

When your Drives, Needs, and Awards are all being met, you are in what I call "the Achievement Zone." It's like the illuminating fusion of battery, wire, and incandescent bulb. You absolutely light up! However, when just two of your three motivational factors are engaged—for instance, your Drive and your Need—you can be reasonably content but you will not feel completely fulfilled.

Let's say your motivational type is "CSI"—you have a Connection Drive, a Stability Need, and an Internal Award system. As an Internal, you are motivated by the knowledge that what you do makes a positive difference. Now let's suppose that you are in a stable job that allows you to work with a friendly group of like-minded people. In other words, two of your three motivators overlap—your Connection Drive and your Stability Need. But let's say that your job does nothing to affect or influence people in a positive way. You do your job well, but you don't feel as if it matters. In that scenario, it is impossible for you to feel genuinely fulfilled. You can still do your job successfully, and even enjoy many aspects of it, but you won't really light up over the work you do. As a result, your motivation level will be muted and you will not experience the passion and bliss of being in your career sweet spot.

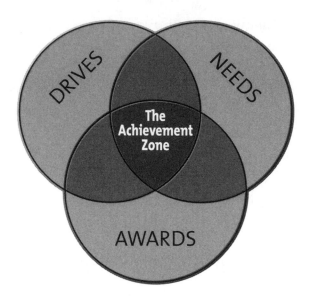

In the illustration above, I've drawn our Drives, Needs, and Awards as overlapping circles. The real sweet spot of high-energy motivation is the dark-shaded area that I call the Achievement Zone—the place where work is fun and success is effortless. But you can get there only when the Drives, Needs, and Awards of your Motivational DNA are all being met.

THE KEY TO EFFORTLESS ACHIEVEMENT

From my research, I can tell you that only about 15 percent of people intuitively know what their Motivational DNA is and are able to utilize that knowledge to their advantage. Most people have only a vague sense of what motivates them and are even more clueless about how to effectively energize others. In the next few chapters, I am going to show you exactly how to identify your Motivational DNA. You'll also learn how to motivate yourself, your coworkers, friends, family members, and others using the principles of Motivational DNA. You will discover how to use strategies that are compatible with your motivational type to achieve outstanding results in every area of your life—physically, financially, emotionally, at work, and at home.

As you begin to consciously motivate yourself in the way that you were designed to be motivated, you will experience remarkable advancements in your career and personal life. Goals that eluded you in the past will be accomplished with ease. And when you learn how to motivate others using this method, people who were once difficult or indifferent will transform before your very eyes. They will become easy to work with, excited to learn, and eager to achieve. The ramifications of this are enormous. It affects absolutely everything that you do and every single person you come into contact with.

In Chapter 2, we're going to decipher your motivational code. And I promise that you won't need to be a scientist to figure it out. Let's get started!

FREE BONUS #1

**Unlimited Online Usage of the Motivational DNA
Profile Tool™ plus a telephone coaching session with one of
Tamara's GET MOTIVATED coaches. ($249 value)**

I want this book to add value to your life in a way that no book has ever done before. Starting right now, I am going to give you a free gift at the end of every chapter in this book! In all, you are going to receive 16 free gifts—including organizational tools, an interactive webinar, audio teachings from the world's greatest celebrity achievers, personal success coaching, special reports, executive summaries of bestselling books, free tickets to my Get Motivated Seminar—and much more!

The retail value of these gifts totals more than $1,800. It's my way of saying thank you for investing in yourself by purchasing this book. I sincerely appreciate the time you are taking to read *Get Motivated!*, and I am determined to ensure that you get *far more than you expected* from this book.

My first gift to you is found online at www.GetMotivatedBook.com. It is a Motivational DNA profile that only takes a few minutes to complete. This online assessment tool will automatically calculate the results of your Motivational DNA profile. It will tell you exactly what motivates you and what de-motivates or discourages you. You'll also get several tips for goal achievement, based on your type. It is my pleasure to give you unlimited access and usage to this testing tool so that you can use it for yourself, coworkers, friends and family members—as often as you like. Additionally, I am going to give you a telephone coaching session with one of my Get Motivated coaches to help you interpret your results and utilize them for your personal and professional success.

What Motivates You?

Now that we've discussed the six factors that comprise Motivational DNA—Connection vs. Production (our Drives); Stability vs. Variety (our Needs); and Internal vs. External Incentives (our Awards)—it's time to assess your unique achievement pattern.

While everyone is motivated by all six factors of Motivational DNA, we each have individual preferences or tendencies among these motivators. This is true for you, your spouse, your friends, your children, your coworkers, and your clients. To most effectively motivate yourself, or anyone else, you need to crack the code of Motivational DNA.

The following twenty-one-question test will reveal your main motivators and decode your Motivational DNA. If you prefer to do this evaluation online, you can go to www.GetMotivatedBook.com and it will automatically calculate your test results.

MOTIVATIONAL DNA PROFILE TOOL

This diagnostic consists of twenty-one pairs of statements that will determine your primary motivational type. Choose the statement in each pair that best describes you as you have been throughout most of your life. Put an "x" in the circle to the right of the statement you have selected. At times, you may feel that both statements are equally true about you, but if you were forced to choose between the two, which statement more accurately reflects your past thoughts and behaviors? If you reflect carefully, you will find that one of the statements has been truer of you than the other. It is best not to overanalyze your choices. You will get more accurate results if you answer spontaneously rather than overthinking your answers.

		A	B	C	D	E	F
1.	I am a supportive, friendly person who seeks intimacy with others.			○			
	I am an achievement-oriented person who seeks to excel.	○					
2.	I tend to be spontaneous and adventurous.						○
	I tend to be methodical and cautious.				○		
3.	I want to be rewarded for excellent work.				○		
	I need to do work that is important to me.		○				
4.	I can come across as being unsure of myself.			○			
	I can come across as being too sure of myself.	○					
5.	I like it when my life is fast-paced, intense, and exciting.						○
	I like it when my life is unhurried, stable, and peaceful.				○		
6.	I prefer public recognition to private recognition.					○	
	I prefer private recognition to public recognition.		○				
7.	I am careful and try to prepare for unforeseen problems.				○		
	I am creative and prefer to improvise as problems come up.						○

	A	B	C	D	E	F
8. Most of the time, I enjoy taking the lead.	●					
Most of the time, I prefer letting someone else lead.			●			
9. I have pursued work that had considerable potential for financial success and personal recognition.				●		
I am willing to forgo financial reward and personal recognition if it means doing work that makes a significant positive difference.		●				
10. Basically, I am laid-back, open, and agreeable.			●			
Basically, I am hard-driving, assertive, and confident.	●					
11. Acquiring the finer things of life is extremely important to me.					●	
Acquiring the finer things of life is not very important to me.		●				
12. I have tended to be focused and disciplined.				●		
I have tended to be impulsive and daring.						●
13. I make things happen.	●					
Whatever will be will be.			●			
14. I don't like dealing with details.						●
I enjoy managing details.				●		
15. Leaving a legacy of contribution to mankind is important to me.		●				
Acquiring wealth and respect is important to me.					●	
16. I'd rather fit in than stand out.			●			
I'd rather stand out than fit in.	●					

	A	B	C	D	E	F
17. I'm interested in maintaining my stability and peace of mind.				●		
I'm interested in challenging myself by doing new things.						●
18. When considering a new job, pay and perks are a primary issue.					●	
When considering a new job, the work itself is a primary issue.			●			
19. I like to challenge the status quo and shake things up.	●					
I like to comfort people and calm them down.				●		
20. What others think of me is very important.		●				
As long as I am true to myself, what others think is not important.					●	
21. Coming up with new ideas and getting people excited about them is one of my major strengths.						●
Implementing ideas and ensuring procedures are followed is one of my major strengths.				●		
Please total each of your columns:						

Is the total of column A or C higher? _____

Circle the italicized word that applies to you.

If the number in column A is higher, you are a *Producer.*

If the number in column C is higher, you are a *Connector.*

Is the total of column D or F higher? _____

Circle the italicized word that applies to you.

If the number in column D is higher, you are a *Stabilizer.*

If the number in column F is higher, you are a *Variable.*

Is the total of column B or E higher? _____

Circle the italicized word that applies to you.

If the number in column B is higher, you are a *Internal.*

If the number in column E is higher, you are a *External.*

RESULTS

Take the first letter of each of the circled words on the left and add them in the boxes below.

Your Motivational DNA type is:

____ ____ ____

You have now identified your primary Motivational DNA type. In the next few chapters, you will learn how you can utilize this knowledge to motivate yourself, your coworkers, your spouse, your friends, and family members of every type.

Part One of this book will show you how the different DNA components combine, and how to fully evaluate yourself and others. You'll also learn how these different elements work together to shape how you are motivated. You will discover how your type differs from other types and learn how to motivate those with codes that are different from yours—especially codes that are 180 degrees opposite of yours.

In Part Two, we will explore the six key factors of Motivational DNA in depth. You'll discover exactly what motivates and de-motivates your type—and every other type. You'll learn how each type thinks, how to best work with them, communicate with them, resolve conflicts, and inspire and lead them. In a nutshell, this section will show you how to bring out the best in yourself and in others.

Part Three will give you the keys to motivating children of every age and motivational style. You'll learn the best motivators for every stage of childhood, and you'll learn how to inspire academic achievement, shape a cooperative, positive attitude, and raise confident, self-motivated children.

Finally, in Part Four, we will break down the essential components of strategic goal achievement as you learn the best ways to start strong, sustain the action, and finish first in every endeavor.

Now I want to give you a brief overview of your particular motivational style. In the following pages, you'll find the eight motivational types, along with some quick-start tips for utilizing your Motivational DNA. Then, in the next few chapters, I am going to show you how to put this powerful system to work to motivate yourself and others.

After locating your type on page 34, you can go directly to Chapter 3, where I will show you how to use your Motivational DNA to accomplish your goals more quickly and easily than you ever imagined possible.

PSI: THE DIRECTOR

YOUR MOTIVATIONAL DNA TYPE IS PSI (PRODUCTION-STABILITY-INTERNAL)

Directors are strategic thinkers who have the ability to move projects forward. They have an eye for detail and energy for execution. Directors are practical and responsible. They are bottom-line people who like to get to the point. Directors are task-oriented and great problem solvers. They are good with schedules, systems, and organization. They focus on achievement and value results. Directors excel in organizations that allow them some autonomy. They know that they bring value to their companies and they need to feel genuinely appreciated for their contributions. Directors are mission-minded and want their work to make a positive contribution.

PSI MOTIVATORS: Freedom from unnecessary constraints, an ability to manage their own time, recognition from their colleagues and peers, an opportunity for personal growth, organized structure, and receiving specific, positive feedback.

PSI DE-MOTIVATORS: Fuzzy goals, coworkers who don't pull their own weight, "groupthink," and the inability to manage their own time and find their own solutions.

Quick-Start Tips for Achieving Your Goals

1. Weak goals don't inspire Directors. Set goals that are both meaningful and challenging.
2. You are energized by challenge. If you can, compete. But make sure you are competing for something that is important to you. For example, if you want to get in shape, train for a marathon that will benefit your favorite charity.
3. Maintaining consistency and establishing accountability will help you accomplish your goals. Craft a plan that provides a steady routine and moves you daily toward your goal. Then track the plan. Using tools like spreadsheets and calendars will help you to be accountable and provide a further impetus for action.

PVI: THE VISIONARY

YOUR MOTIVATIONAL DNA TYPE IS PVI (PRODUCTION-VARIETY-INTERNAL)

Visionaries are persistent, energetic, and confident. They are able to organize people and projects. They exhibit strong leadership potential and react quickly to crisis. Creative thinkers, Visionaries have the ability to craft a vision and get others excited about it. They enjoy working on multiple projects at the same time and like to be involved in exploring alternative concepts. Farsighted and imaginative, Visionaries are good at finding original solutions to difficult problems. Visionaries enjoy change and thrive under pressure. They have the ability to shift gears and turn on a dime. They are confident in their ability to master new skills. Visionaries enjoy challenge and desire personal growth. Visionaries want to know that their work matters and desire to "go where no man has gone before."

PVI MOTIVATORS: An inspiring work environment, the opportunity to originate and initiate ideas, peer respect, credit for work done, and a strong sense of mission.

PVI DE-MOTIVATORS: Rigid structure, monotonous routine, delays, time-consuming details, and bureaucracy.

Quick-Start Tips for Achieving Your Goals

1. It is vital that you have options. Make a list of a dozen ways to accomplish your goal. Then mix it up. Do a little of everything on the list. PVI Visionaries tire quickly of the same old, same old.

2. Create a specific plan for achieving your objectives. If something doesn't work for you, don't force yourself to do it—eliminate it. Find a better way—something more enjoyable or exciting.

3. Make a detailed record of why your goal is important to you. How will you (and others) benefit if you achieve your goal? What are the consequences if you don't?

PSE: THE CHIEF

YOUR MOTIVATIONAL DNA TYPE IS PSE
(PRODUCTION-STABILITY-EXTERNAL)

Chiefs have a strong desire for tangible results combined with a need for precision. Chiefs are determined and strong-minded. They are independent and able to work unsupervised with good results. Chiefs can make quick decisions, but prefer to do so when they first have all the facts. They enjoy having the authority to chart their own course. They have considerable organizational ability and are able to develop systems and procedures easily. Chiefs feel validated and esteemed by tangible benefits. They methodically work toward goals that offer significant, concrete rewards. They are "mission accomplished" people with a need to achieve specific objectives.

PSE MOTIVATORS: Autonomy, public recognition, special privileges, freedom from unnecessary controls, the ability to structure their environment to their liking, time to think, the power to act, and acknowledgment of their special skills and achievements.

PSE DE-MOTIVATORS: Rigidity or control from supervisors or authority figures, inefficient systems, and ineffective people.

Quick-Start Tips for Achieving Your Goals

1. Consistency is essential for your motivational type. It's better to do a little something toward your goal each day than to have a series of starts and stops.
2. Clearly define your goal, break it down into manageable pieces, and set a deadline for completion.
3. From the outset, plan rewards for incremental achievement—and make sure that they are significant and highly desirable.

PVE: THE CHAMPION

YOUR MOTIVATIONAL DNA TYPE IS PVE (PRODUCTION-VARIETY-EXTERNAL)

Champions enjoy a challenge and love to win. They are charming and enthusiastic leaders. Champions are natural persuaders. They don't mind being the center of attention and are good at working with others while advancing their own ideas. Champions tend to be engaging and charismatic. They are skilled at getting things done in spite of seemingly insurmountable obstacles. In fact, obstacles just make tasks more interesting for a Champion. They are quick decision makers and can be impatient with those who are not. As solid negotiators, Champions are willing to compromise to get the job done. Champions have an innate ability to get others to follow their lead.

PVE MOTIVATORS: Challenging assignments, the authority to make decisions, profitability, freedom from supervision and excessive control, opportunities for advancement, deadlines, calculated risk, and popularity.

PVE DE-MOTIVATORS: Strict controls, inability to manage their own time and projects, protracted analysis, and deliberation without meaningful action.

Quick-Start Tips for Achieving Your Goals

1. Your motivational type likes to be busy. It's imperative that you create space in your schedule to devote exclusively to doing what is necessary to achieve your objectives. The time will not magically appear. You must block off periods of time to work on your goals.

2. Competition and commensurate rewards are powerful motiva-

tors for your motivational style. Design a contest with like-minded achievers who have the same goal. The first one to achieve his or her goal wins the prize.

3. Make sure that the process is enjoyable. Invest the time you need to find fun ways to achieve your goal.

CSI: THE SUPPORTER

YOUR MOTIVATIONAL DNA TYPE IS CSI (CONNECTION-STABILITY-INTERNAL)

Supporters are practical, dependable, and loyal. They are both people-oriented and detail-oriented. Supporters are natural supervisors. They thrive on helping others excel in their positions and will fight for the underdog. Methodical in their work, they like to have the facts before they act. They respect authority and organizational structure. Caring and careful with people and projects, Supporters are skillful at implementing procedures. They possess a strong work ethic. Having a clearly defined goal to work toward is important to them, and they follow through on objectives with conscientiousness. Psychological pay is of primary importance to them. They need to feel good about what they are doing and sense that their work makes a positive contribution.

CSI MOTIVATORS: Facts and information, peer respect, sincere appreciation, private recognition, specific positive feedback, an inspiring work environment, coworkers they enjoy, clearly defined objectives, a sense of accomplishment, and time to reflect and plan.

CSI DE-MOTIVATORS: Hype and hyperbole, infringement on personal or family time, perceived inequity, and demands for rapid change.

Quick-Start Tips for Achieving Your Goals

1. Your motivational type can become discouraged by huge goals. For that reason, make sure that your aspirations are realistic. Set manageable goals that can be achieved in a reasonable time frame.

2. Be gentle with yourself. Don't expect perfection. Slow and steady progress should be your expectation.

3. Involve others. Make a list of the people, organizations, and resources that will assist you in achieving your goal. Supporters excel when they are working toward an individual and team goal with others who are equally committed to achievement.

CVI: THE RELATER

YOUR MOTIVATIONAL DNA TYPE IS CVI (CONNECTION-VARIETY-INTERNAL)

Relaters are caring and creative. They relish life and cherish relationships. Relaters are outgoing, friendly, and well liked. They are resourceful and inventive, with an ability to compromise to get the job done. They are team players who bring out the best in others. Warm and enthusiastic, they balance concern for others with a zeal for personal growth. Relaters are personal and practical in their approach to problem solving. They have an innate ability to create win-win solutions. Relaters value what is really important and desire to make a positive contribution to society. Blending loyalty with adventure, Relaters are fun friends and devoted partners.

CVI MOTIVATORS: Genuine appreciation for a job done well, opportunities for personal growth, fun coworkers, teamwork, new experiences, and an inspiring work environment.

CVI DE-MOTIVATORS: Isolation, rigid routine, pressure-cooker deadlines, quenching creativity, disapproval, and conflict.

Quick-Start Tips for Achieving Your Goals

1. You are a people person, so the best way for you to achieve your objectives is to collaborate with a partner or group of people who share the same purpose. Find or create a support group that will cheer you on until you reach your goal.
2. Follow-through is a challenge for your motivational style. You must become accountable to your goal and do something each day, no matter how small, that moves you closer to your target.
3. Take some time to soul-search and ask yourself why your goal is important. Write down those reasons and refer to them often. It is the "why," not the "how," that inspires your motivational type.

CSE: THE REFINER

YOUR MOTIVATIONAL DNA TYPE IS CSE (CONNECTION-STABILITY-EXTERNAL)

Refiners are systematic thinkers who value precision. They have the ability to see the big picture while still focusing on the details. Refiners are conscientious and disciplined. They are supportive and respectful of others. Personal and practical, Refiners tend to be family-oriented. They are deeply loyal and have a well-defined sense of right and wrong. They prefer a "democratic" style of leadership and expect others to play according to the rules. Refiners are dependable and diligent. Fair pay and sincere appreciation for their work make them feel valued. They are deliberate in their decision making and want to ensure that their choices do not adversely affect others.

CSE MOTIVATORS: Having all the facts as well as enough time to analyze them, competent team members, recognition by superiors, special privileges, freedom from controls, and genuine respect.

CSE DE-MOTIVATORS: High-pressure deadlines, too many cooks in the kitchen, rapid change, infringement on personal or family time and perceived inequity.

Quick-Start Tips for Achieving Your Goals

1. Your motivational style excels when you are coached by a mentor. Interview people who have already accomplished your dream and find out how they did it. Ask them to assist and advise you when you run into problems along the way.
2. Don't jump into a significant undertaking without first doing due diligence. Research the ideal way to achieve your goal. There is a *best* way—find it.
3. Set aside a significant amount of money each week that you will spend to reward yourself if you meet your goal on time.

CVE: THE EXPLORER

YOUR MOTIVATIONAL DNA TYPE IS CVE (CONNECTION-VARIETY-EXTERNAL)

Explorers are animated and spontaneous, with a love for adventure. They are perceptive, insightful, and very good at reading people. Warm, considerate, and thoughtful, Explorers light up in social situations. Explorers bring out the best in others by encouraging and appreciating them. They are creative problem solvers and are skilled at finding unique solutions. Explorers foster cooperation and are good at getting others to collaborate. They value hard work—but they want their work to be fun and rewarding. Explorers like jobs that give them the opportunity to learn new skills and meet new people.

CVE MOTIVATORS: Simulating relationships, opportunities for personal growth and advancement within the organization, freedom to do things their way, esteem, good compensation and bonuses.

CVE DE-MOTIVATORS: Routine, bureaucracy, isolation, disapproval, and the quenching of creativity.

Quick-Start Tips for Achieving Your Goals

1. Camaraderie is the key for your motivational type. Involving others will help you stay fired up about your goal. Even the most unpleasant tasks are fun for you when people you enjoy are a part of the plan.
2. Explorers need choices. There is always more than one way to achieve a goal. Create an exhaustive list of all the ways that have worked for others and endeavor to try everything on the list.
3. Reward yourself along the way. Celebrate even your small successes and splurge on a big reward when you complete your goal.

FREE BONUS #2
Two VIP Tickets to See Tamara Lowe *live and in-person*
at a GET MOTIVATED Business Seminar. ($600 Value)

The *Philadelphia Inquirer* really said it best, "You may have attended business seminars before, but you've never seen anything like this. Secrets, formulas, and wisdom. A gust of inspiration and a brush with celebrity. There's something for everyone." This is your chance to experience what the *Washington Post* calls "The Super Bowl of Success!"

To access your free gifts from this point on, please go online to www.GetMotivatedBook.com/gifts and register by 12/31/09 using the official offer code printed in the box on the back flap of the book jacket.

The Success Strategies of Highly Motivated Achievers

According to Gallup polls, a lack of employee motivation in our nation's workforce costs the U.S. economy up to $370 billion every year. The *Wall Street Journal* reports that unmotivated employees tend to be less happy, less healthy, and less focused than motivated employees, resulting in higher health-care expenditures for employers, lower productivity, increased absenteeism, and more on-the-job accidents.[1] Insufficient motivation holds people back in their careers and holds our companies back in the marketplace.

Motivation, or the lack of it, affects our children as well. The phrase "a crisis of motivation" has become common terminology among educators. The National Education Association says that more than half of new teachers leave the profession in the first five years, discouraged by unmotivated, uninterested students.

On the positive side, numerous studies suggest that motivation may be the prescription for a healthy life. Motivated patients recover faster following surgery, have more successful rehabilitations, and show a 40–75 percent reduction in health-care costs compared to less motivated patients.[2,3]

The Economic Impact of Motivation

Motivation is an essential factor behind financial success, as well. People who consider themselves "very motivated" earn an average of $44,108 more annually than those who consider themselves "unmotivated." The motivated group also expressed significantly higher levels of personal happiness than the unmotivated group.

As all of these statistics highlight, increased motivation can improve the quality of our lives financially, physically, and emotionally. When people are inspired to live up to their full potential, they excel—and so do their companies. Motivated people are more fulfilled and productive. They enjoy life more. As you discover how you were truly meant to be motivated, it can have a profoundly positive effect on your sense of fulfillment, both on and off the job.

Understanding Your Motivational Triggers

When my friend Jim Wilson cracked the code of his Motivational DNA, it completely transformed his life. He began to rethink his role as keeper of the norms and decided to make a radical change. After seventeen years in hotel management, Jim left the profession to become an airboat guide in the Florida Everglades. Jim traded a well-paying position, with seniority, security, and clout, for a job that has him mucking around in swamp water ten hours a day—and he has never been happier.

While the perks of Jim's management job would be wonderful motivators for other motivational types, Jim is a CVI; what energizes him has little to do with salary and perks. Recently, Jim took my family on a wild airboat ride. As we flew through the breathtaking beauty of the Everglades at breakneck speeds, Jim was clearly having the time of his life. Afterward, he gave us a tour of the wildlife refuge where he works, identifying the cypress trees, saw grass, and mangroves. He pointed out the water birds native to the swampland and showed us the nursery where baby alligators are hatched.

"I wish you had been here yesterday," he said. "You missed all the fun. An eight-foot-long alligator tried to crawl into my boat! We had to capture the gator and move him to the other side of the park."

Pointing to his partner, Jim said, "I'm 170 pounds and my buddy Ray is 210. This bad boy was flipping us around like it was nothing! Thankfully, we got his mouth taped up, but it wasn't easy."

"And this is better than hotel management?" I asked incredulously.

"Are you kidding? I hated all the backstabbing, politics, and pressures of management. At least in the Everglades the predators can be contained."

As we spoke, this former corporate professional stood knee-deep in the marsh water, covered in mud, and was grinning like a gator himself.

"I love this job!" Jim said. "I love coming to work. I never look at my watch. I wish I'd left hotel management years ago!"

For Jim, it wasn't a sacrifice to give up the status or security of his former occupation, because those things are not what he desired most in the first place. Unfortunately, it took him seventeen years to figure that out.

As Jim's experience demonstrates, when you unlock your motivational code it can have a huge impact on the sense of fulfillment and joy you experience in your life, both personally and professionally.

Developing a Core Competency

I love to watch people who are proficient in their work, whether they are a cashier or an athlete, a sign painter or a politician. Inevitably, such people are motivated—they have discovered the secret to living in the Achievement Zone.

Recently, during a connection at the Dallas–Fort Worth Airport, I took an electric cart to my gate, which was in another terminal. I've taken carts a few times over the years, but this occasion was memorable because my driver, Franklin, was a world-class chauffeur. Most airport cart drivers seem bored or vaguely irritated. They bellow, "Excuse the cart," but you have the distinct impression that what they're really thinking is, *When you hear the loud beeping noise behind you—get out of the way, you idiot!* Not Franklin! He left a path of smiling faces in his wake as he breezed through the corridors, calling out greetings, cracking jokes, and weaving adeptly past pedestrians. From the quick, efficient way that he loaded luggage to his joyous interactions with passengers, he had taken a basic task and turned it into an art form. Seeing Franklin in action is just plain fun to watch.

Although it sounds a bit odd, I get an equal amount of pleasure from being "sold" by a competent salesperson. I have taught sales and negotiation skills for decades, so I immediately recognize a professional. I can't help but respond when an expert salesperson "qualifies" me (determines whether I am a likely candidate for his or her product or service), discovers my needs, and showcases the benefits of the product. I am secretly delighted to watch the sales pro overcome my objections one by one, shooting them down like metal ducks at a county fair.

It's a thing of beauty to behold the skilled salesperson go in for the close, then put a cherry on top by requesting referrals. An expert salesperson *compels* me to buy. I barely have a choice in the matter. I want to reward him or her simply for becoming a master of the craft.

I mention these examples because it is my hope that you will not just experiment with Motivational DNA, but you will learn to master it so that it becomes a core competency for you. I urge you to practice the strategies that I am going to outline in the next few chapters until they become second nature. If you do, then it will enhance every aspect of your life and work.

Being properly motivated is the difference between being an average violinist and a virtuoso. Both make music, but the master musician achieves awe-inspiring results. How do you develop mastery in Motivational DNA? You invest yourself in the process. The more you invest in developing the skills you need to motivate yourself and others, the greater your rewards will be.

Focus on the Factors

I'm a bit of a skeptic. I only buy into concepts that I have thoroughly tested myself. If a new management theory or business trend comes along, I check it out. I experiment with it to prove whether or not it works in real life. In the case of Motivational DNA, I can tell you from personal experience that it works.

As I look back on my life, I can see that I struggled or failed in areas where I had used motivational strategies that were incompatible with my Motivational DNA. When I succeeded, it was because I had unknowingly used strategies that were well suited to my motivational makeup. Understanding my Motivational DNA has given me the freedom to build on my strengths and offset my imperfections. It enables me to organize my life in a way that makes me, and those around me, happier and more effective.

My Motivational DNA type is PVI (The Visionary). I have a strong Production Drive, an extremely high Variety Need, and an Internal Award system. My dominant motivational factor is Variety.

At this point, I want to caution you not to be too concerned about trying to remember the various types of Motivational DNA. You might think it is important to commit these combinations to memory, but it's not and here's why. Whether you are a PVI Visionary, like me, or a CSE Refiner, or any other type, one thing remains the same—everyone is motivated by *all six* factors of Motivational DNA to varying degrees. It is the individual factors of Motivational DNA (Production, Connection, Stability, Variety, Internal Awards, and External Awards), not the specific combination of these motivators, that are the most important thing to focus on.

The Six Things That Motivate Everyone

It is not vital to know exactly how your type interacts with someone else's motivational type. What's crucial is to be able to recognize the six components of Motivational DNA when you see someone operating in them. Then you will know how to adapt your behavior and style of communication in order to effectively motivate the other person. In the following chapters, we will delve more deeply into the six motivational factors to help you get a firm handle on each of them and recognize the signs of them in others.

As I mentioned in Chapter 1, our motivational tendencies may shift in various settings. In one environment you're one way, and in another environment you may act differently. In fact, you may have had trouble answering the questions in the motivational profile because you might have a high Production Drive in one setting and an almost equally high Connection Drive in another. Right now it is not critical for you to gauge those distinctions. Here's what I want you to remember: *Your primary motivational type is key when you want to motivate yourself.* However, when you are motivating others, your own motivational type is irrelevant. All that matters at that point is *their* motivational type. You have to mesh your style to theirs.

Let me give you a few examples from my life to illustrate how to use Motivational DNA. Along the way, I will teach you three powerful strategies for utilizing this system to achieve your goals, overcome obstacles, and increase your quality of life.

Motivational DNA at Work

As a college student, I labored in a number of odd jobs as I put myself through school. I was a waitress, a doctor's receptionist, and a grocery store cashier. After college, I worked in the hotel and banking industries. Today, I am the co-founder and executive vice president of a large educational organization. Over the past thirty years, my responsibilities have changed many times, but one aspect about me has remained the same: I have always disliked company meetings.

Conventional business wisdom says that in order to mobilize a team to action, committees should be convened, options discussed, strategies planned, tasks assigned, and so forth. I don't dispute that and I think it's sound counsel. But I've discovered that it just doesn't work well for me. Although I love people, I do not have a high Connection drive and I am extremely unmotivated when it comes to conference room deliberations. Connectors have an endless capacity for such planning sessions. I envy that, but I personally can't stand those types of meetings. It tends to frustrate me when discussions ramble and veer off topic. However, since conferences are a necessary evil in corporate life, I have devised a strategy that works for my motivational profile.

In my organization, I have learned to let the Connectors connect and the Producers produce. My direct reports are primarily Producers. Of course, we assemble to discuss business, but our meetings tend to be brief and to the point. I consciously organize my Connectors, on the other hand, into groups and teams. Connectors are wired to perform better when they link up with other Connectors. When I attend meetings with Connectors I often multitask by taking notes, asking questions, listening, affirming, answering correspondence, and purging e-mail. That way my Connectors feel good about having me in the room to bounce ideas off of and help make decisions, and I am more patient and unhurried with them.

I am a true believer in the inexhaustible capacity of human beings to learn and develop. Every skill is a learnable skill. Yet we are also subject to inborn limitations. For example, Tom Brady is an exceptionally talented athlete. The 6′3″ star quarterback of the New England Patriots has a rocket arm, laser vision, and stunning passing accuracy, but he would be an utter failure as a jockey. Now, this doesn't mean he can't ride a horse. It may not be his strength, but like all of us, he has the ability to incorporate many behaviors that may fall outside of his natural gifts.

STRATEGY #1: GENE SPLICING

In the next chapter, I am going to give you more insights on how to motivate others. But for now I'd like to introduce a concept called *gene splicing*. This is the ability to adopt traits from other motivational types in order to expand your own behavioral repertoire. Gene splicing gives you the power to vary your behavior in order to better connect with another person. Rather than repeating behaviors that are ineffective, gene splicing allows you to "borrow" traits from the motivational grid that do not come naturally to you.

In genetics, gene splicing involves cutting the DNA of a gene to join it together with genetic material from another entity. It is similar to cutting and splicing videotape together. The goal of gene splicing is to introduce new characteristics or attributes that will enhance existing ones. Similarly, we can use the concept of gene splicing in Motivational DNA to introduce new motivational traits that will enhance our natural tendencies.

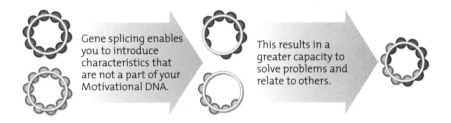

Gene splicing enables you to introduce characteristics that are not a part of your Motivational DNA.

This results in a greater capacity to solve problems and relate to others.

Let me give you an example of how behavioral gene splicing works. Connectors are motivated by a drive for relationship. They like to bond and spend time with their coworkers. If you are a Producer, as I am, your drive for relationships may be relatively low. By using the concept of gene splicing, however, you can expand your emotional repertoire to include behaviors that will resonate with and nurture Connectors. What do I mean by that? My point is that you can learn how to slow down, make eye contact, really listen to them, demonstrate concern for their needs, and show interest in the things they care about. Behaviors that are outside of your Motivational DNA type may not come naturally to you, but you can *consciously* adopt these patterns as you interact with people who have different motivational types.

Similarly, Connectors can use the concept of gene splicing to enhance their relationships with those who are Producers—for example, by amping up how fast they communicate and do things. It's simply a matter of temporarily borrowing or adopting attitudes and aptitudes from another motivational type. While behaviors outside of your Motivational DNA may not be innate or effortless, everyone is capable of consciously adapting their behaviors when necessary.

Here is another example. As a rule, Producers want to know the bottom line first. Then, and only then, will they be patient enough to allow you to fill in the details. It's not that Producers are uninterested in details; it's just that they are *more interested* in the end result. They want to see the equation like this:

"THE ANSWER IS 100. I ARRIVED AT THIS CONCLUSION BY ADDING 50 + 50."

Connectors, however, are wired with a different algorithm. To describe the calculation as $100 = 50 + 50$ may seem too blunt to a Connector. Connectors want to hear how you first encountered the problem, who else was involved in the working out the computation, the basic sequence of steps you went through, and the various difficulties that you faced along the way. That method of communication drives Producers mad. If you are a Connector, you'll need to speed up your communications—and edit them down—when dealing with Producers. If you are a Producer, you'll need to do just the opposite—slow down, engage in social niceties, elaborate on the details, and let your Connectors feel the love.

When I have trouble motivating one of my children or an employee at work, I ask myself, "How can I use this person's Motivational DNA to solve the problem?" Then I adopt, or splice, the traits from their type that will help me to motivate them.

Motivational DNA and Goal Achievement

A few years ago, I had a sports injury that sidelined me for more than a year. During that time, I was unable to exercise. As a result, I gained a pound a month. That may not seem like a lot, but I am 5′5″ (when I lie). Every pound shows up as two pounds on me. Once I had the doctor's okay, I started exercising again. But those fifteen pounds had no intention of melting away. I've always had to be diligent about watching my weight, but this time the weight would not come off. I exercised, dieted, and cursed my misfortune, but no matter what I did, the scale would not budge. It was extremely frustrating to me to spend months focused on losing weight with no real progress to show for my efforts. After a while, I was forced to own up to what was holding me back: I was not really motivated to lose weight. I didn't like being overweight, but I didn't have the unwavering commitment that I needed to do anything about it. Finally I asked myself, *Can I solve this problem using Motivational DNA?*

STRATEGY #2: APPEAL TO YOUR MOTIVATORS

To answer this question, I went through a two-step process. First, I listed my main motivators on a sheet of paper. Second, I devised a plan of action that was compatible with each of my motivational preferences. This easy exercise requires very little time. Here's how the process played out:

I wrote, "I am a Producer." Then I thought about what motivates a Producer.

Producers love to win and hate to lose. I realized the thing that would motivate me best would be competition. I wondered, *Is there such a thing as an online weight-loss competition?* I logged on to a search engine and typed in "weight-loss competition." I immediately found a Web site that had launched a public weight-loss competition and I entered the contest.

Next, I wrote, "I am a Variable," and then I reflected on what motivates Variables.

Variables are completely unmotivated by repetitive structure. Stabilizers tend to do well with diets, because they provide the order that Stabilizers crave. Diets weren't working for me because they demand conformity to an inflexible set of rules. I decided to count calories so that I could eat whatever I wanted. Chocolate, cheese, pasta . . . nothing would be forbidden. Once again, I looked online for support. I found a Web site that allowed me to track my calories on a daily basis and also accounted for the calories I burned during exercise. I resolved to eat 300 calories less than I normally took in each day—the equivalent of half a sandwich—or burn 300 calories more through exercise. The key was to give myself variety, options, and freedom.

Finally, I wrote down my award system: "I am an Internal." Then I thought about what might motivate an Internal to lose weight.

While External rewards like compliments and new clothes are nice for some people, Internals are not highly motivated by those kinds of things. I decided to make a list of Internal awards that would help me stay mentally motivated. My list included such things as having more energy and clarity, reducing stress, improving my strength, flexibility, health, and sense of well-being. All of these were strong motivators for me, especially when I factored in the increased ability to keep up with my children and my husband, who is an extremely energetic person.

The Power of Intentional Focus

This planning process took less than fifteen minutes. All I did was appeal to each of my primary motivational factors and create well-suited incentives for my motivational type. The result? In three months I lost fifteen pounds—10 percent of my body weight. I also won first place in the contest. In fact, it worked so well that I joined a second fitness competition and lost an additional ten pounds over the next three months, and won first place in that contest as well!

You may be thinking, *That sounds so simple.* Can I tell you the truth? It *was* so simple! The best solutions are usually not bogged down by clutter and complexity. The only difficulty I encountered was the amount of time I wasted trying to lose weight without utilizing my Motivational DNA. That was a miserable ordeal. It was incredibly demotivating. Once I tapped into my motivational profile, the whole process was painless. In fact, it was fun! Yes, Motivational DNA really works! The beauty of the system is that it works for everyone who uses it. Motivational DNA will work for you, too. And before this chapter is over, we are going to tackle one of your toughest goals.

Using Motivational DNA in a Crisis Situation

Five years ago, I took a vacation with my best friend, Lindsey—it's one that I will never forget. My friend and I decided to get as far away from the stress of daily life as we possibly could. We chose a tropical island in the Caribbean. Lindsey and I were eager to take a break from the pressures of work and family responsibilities and enjoy a girls' getaway. The island we went to was a dream, a Caribbean paradise. The weather was postcard perfect and the scenery spectacular. We rented a beautiful beach house and spent our first evening by the pool. We stayed up late that night—well past midnight—laughing and chatting. Finally, I decided to call it a night.

"Sweetie, I'm spent! I'm going to bed," I said. "See you in the morning!"

As I started down the hall to my bedroom, I thought I heard footsteps and whispers. *It must be my imagination*, I thought. Suddenly, two men wearing ski masks exploded from the room. One of the men seized me and the other overpowered my friend. The gunmen shouted profanities and spat out demands. I wasn't sure what they wanted and had no time to react.

"Where are your husbands? Where is the [expletive] gold? Who's in the [expletive] house? Give us the gold!"

I tried to formulate answers as I watched my friend melt down before my eyes. She screamed and howled, thrashing in all directions. One of the men locked her in a choke hold and put a revolver to her temple. "Shut up now or I'll shoot you! I'll kill you both!" he shrieked.

I reached out and grabbed Lindsey's arm. "Calm down! It's all right. We're okay!" I said. To my great relief, Lindsey relaxed.

I turned to the gunman who had seized me and looked him in the eye. I remember thinking, *This is someone's little boy.* As odd as it sounds, my main emotion at that moment was not fear, but compassion for the troubled young men who threatened our lives.

"This is your show," I said. "We're the only ones here. Our husbands are not on the island. Please don't hurt us. We'll give you whatever you need."

"We want the [expletive] gold! Where is it?"

"I don't know who told you we have gold, but they gave you bad information. We can give you cash. We've got cell phones and computers. But we don't have anything else."

"Give us the [expletive] cash! Where are the [expletive] computers?" the man shrieked in my ear.

Suddenly, I felt bold—and more than a little annoyed. I said, "Listen to me! We are going to help you because we are Christians. We will give you whatever valuables we have just to bless you. You are not taking it from us—we are giving it to you. However, you are still a guest in this house and I forbid you from using foul language. I don't want to hear any more profanity out of you. You will speak to us with respect."

The gunman holding me began trembling. I could feel him shaking as he held me by the arm and neck. He turned to his partner and said, "Come on, man! Let's just get out of here!"

Lindsey's purse was on a chair next to the man who had attacked her.

"Lindsey, give him your wallet," I said. The gunman released his grip on her. As Lindsey handed over her money, she smiled and said, "God bless you."

We gave the men our cash, computers, cell phones, and jewelry. And the men did not utter one more expletive in our presence. Eventually, they ran off. The whole episode lasted perhaps thirty minutes, but, by the grace of God, we were not harmed in any way. We later learned that these two men had raped a woman two days earlier when they broke into her home. Three weeks later, one of the robbers was shot by a homeowner during a break-in and both men were captured.

I wanted to tell you about this experience because Motivational DNA turned out to be key to my recovery following this incident. As a Producer, I have a tendency to try to fix my own problems rather than seek help from others. My coping mechanism in times of crisis can be summed up with the words "Move on." *Get over it. Life is short. Move on.* Yes, I had experienced a terrible trauma. But I had survived uninjured;

I just wanted to get on with my life. I packed my bags, returned home, and intended to get back to business as usual.

In the aftermath of the crime, however, my "move on" mentality simply wasn't enough. I was traumatized on a deep level by being held captive and facing the very real possibility of losing my friend or my own life. For the next eight months, I was jumpy and easily frightened when approached suddenly by strangers. On several occasions when information was demanded of me and I didn't feel I had the right answers, I found it difficult to breathe. I had trouble sleeping at night.

A friend of mine who is a counselor, Dr. Brent Larson, told me that all of these things were normal. He said, "This is similar to what happens when a person is involved in a near-fatal automobile accident. It affects them on a cellular level. For up to two years following the accident, they tend to hit their brakes while driving whenever they see anything in their peripheral vision." Dr. Larson said, "What you are experiencing is a very common response to a traumatic event." While it was comforting to know that my experience was normal, I still just wanted to *move on*. Unfortunately, my Producer strategies didn't work well in this situation. As much as I would have liked to put the matter behind me, I was still undergoing debilitating bouts of fear and anxiety.

Using the insights I had gained though my work with Motivational DNA, I realized I needed to change my game plan. Right after the break-in, I told only a few people about the attack. I didn't want to be perceived as being vulnerable. I didn't want sympathy. I just wanted to get on with my life. But on some level, the trauma of the attack had paralyzed me internally. I didn't realize it, but by staying silent I remained stuck. I needed to process what had happened to me psychologically, spiritually, physically, and emotionally.

Being the kind of independent Producer that I am, I preferred to handle my self-diagnosed post-traumatic stress on my own . . . but I couldn't. Many months passed before I realized that my Producer coping strategies were not helping me. I had to incorporate the concept of gene splicing and adopt Connector strategies in order to heal. Over the course of a week, I contacted more than thirty people who I thought might be able to help me. The outcome was almost miraculous. At that point, I began to make a rapid recovery.

A few years ago, I could not have written about these things. Producers don't like being vulnerable. We tend to dislike exposure, being perceived as overly emotional, or any form of sentiment that hinders production. Producers don't want to hear people whine about their problems, and they certainly don't want to moan about their own troubles. Producers would rather fix the problem than talk about it. In disclosing what I just shared with you, I am stretching myself. Although it's still a bit uncomfortable for me, I must admit that I grew personally as I deliberately adopted Connector strategies to expand my relationships. I've learned to lower my guard and accept help from others. This is one of the life-empowering benefits of Motivational DNA. It can help you enlarge your capacity for growth.

Now It's Your Turn

How can *you* best motivate yourself using Motivational DNA? In just a moment, we will work on one of your goals using this three-step approach:

With a current challenge in mind, you will first create a series of solutions that is compatible with your Motivational DNA.

Next, you will test your solutions, discarding the ones that don't work. You will play to your strengths by using strategies that work.

If you are not getting results by appealing to your Motivational DNA, you will use gene splicing to *adopt* effective strategies from the other types.

People who have behavioral flexibility generally score high in all of the six motivational factors. For example, if you have a high Production Drive and an almost equally high Connection Drive, you can adapt to challenging situations more easily than someone who is high in one area but relatively low in the other. Being strong in both areas enables you to use twice as many success strategies to achieve the outcomes you deserve. For example, you can tackle a goal using Stability strategies or Variety strategies, or a combination of the two. Gene splicing enables you to have the best of both worlds. It allows you to borrow competencies from the other types even if those behaviors don't come naturally to you. At first you will have to do this consciously, but as you gain experience and practice, it will become much easier.

STRATEGY #3: INTENTIONAL FOCUS

As you continue through this book, I am going to give you additional skills and concepts to help you better understand your Motivational DNA. But you can begin using Motivational DNA right now. Here's how to get started: Select your most challenging short-term goal (something that you can realistically accomplish within ninety days), like losing weight, winning a promotion, or planning a renovation. Write it down. You can do that in Appendix A at the back of this book, or open up a blank computer document or spreadsheet and type it there.

Next, answer the questions below for each *of your three primary motivational factors*. Include as much detail as possible for each of your answers. These questions are also listed in Appendix A.

The following questions are designed to help you create a personal plan of attack. They address the obstacles you will encounter, the people and organizations that can assist you, and ways to sustain focus, make the process more enjoyable, organize your plan, and provide inspiration for times when willpower is not enough. After you answer these questions, you will have a dozen strategies and inspirational ideas to help you achieve your goal—and you'll have a plan of action to chart your course. I believe you will find these questions enjoyable to answer because they appeal to your unique combination of motivational traits.

Connectors

- What organizations can I connect with to help me achieve my goal?
- Who has successfully accomplished the same (or a similar) goal and can help me strategize to overcome the obstacles I will encounter?
- What groups can I join to support me and fuel my motivation?
- Who can encourage me to stay on track and help make me accountable?

Producers

- How can I turn this goal into a competition?
- What obstacles and distractions will I need to navigate in order to achieve my goal?
- How will I overcome those obstacles?
- Which people, groups, and organizations can I deploy to help me do the heavy lifting?

Stabilizers

- What existing systems and structures can I utilize to help me reach my goal?
- What can I do now to research and create a methodology that will help me succeed?
- How can I eliminate distractions and focus on doing something every day that will cause me to make progress toward accomplishing my goal?
- How will achieving my goal add balance and stability to my life?

Variables

- What can I do to add fun to the equation and at the same time advance me toward my goal?
- What are the most creative and interesting ways to accomplish my goal?
- If Plan A doesn't work, what will I do for Plans B through Z?
- How will I add variety, joy, and excitement to the process so that I don't get bored?

Internals

- Why is this goal meaningful to me?
- How will it make a positive difference to others?
- What are the things that will keep me from quitting when the going gets tough or the pace becomes tedious?
- What inner resources will I utilize to take action daily toward my goal?

Externals

- How will I personally benefit by achieving this goal?
- What incremental rewards can I build into the process to help me accomplish my goal?
- How does realizing this goal set me up for even greater success?
- What big reward will I give myself when I cross the finish line?

If you are serious about achieving your goal, don't move on to the next chapter until you record your answers to the above questions. Don't simply read the questions and answer them mentally. Invest the time to give thoughtful, detailed answers *in writing*.

Most of us don't attempt anything challenging until we're motivated to do it. But here's the dilemma: We usually don't know how to create the motivation we desire. Instead, we wait until we're inspired.

The problem is that being struck by inspiration is almost as rare as being struck by lightning. In everyday life, it rarely happens. Why wait for inspiration to strike when we can intentionally motivate ourselves? Waiting to be inspired is like sitting in the dark waiting for dawn when you could easily flip on a light switch. With Motivational DNA, generating energy and inspiration is as simple as turning on the lights. All you have to do is use it.

FREE BONUS #3

The Masters of Motivation Audio Coaching Series—18 Super Achievers Share Their Success Secrets with You. ($89 value)

It's impossible to succeed at the highest levels in the world of professional sports without becoming a master of motivation. Over the years I've had the opportunity to record interviews with the greatest sports heroes of our time. Now I'm opening my personal archive to you! This dynamic audio program features the most memorable interview segments from 18 of the greatest athletes and coaches of our time. The lessons they share are as valuable off the field as they are on the field. *The Masters of Motivation* will help you gain the winner's edge and give you the competitive advantage.

Motivating People to Improve Their Performance

I used to think that I was a marvelous judge of character. I thought I could read people and assess their basic qualities in the same way that Superman can see through walls of steel and analyze the chemical composition of substances. But when I confronted the challenge of hiring employees, my illusions of superpowers perished. I discovered that I was actually a shockingly bad judge of character.

The cheerful, friendly receptionist I hired turned out to be a world-class gossipmonger. Before I could uncover her secret identity, she left a charred wasteland in her path, much like an uncontrolled California wildfire.

The confident, competent middle manager I brought on board transformed himself into a Stalinesque prison guard who alienated, offended, and scolded his subordinates, provoking a mass mutiny within weeks of his arrival.

And the energetic, professional salesperson I hired? He turned out to be about as productive as a sprouting potato.

If only I had known about Motivational DNA back then!

The Dollars and Cents of Motivation

In business, motivation is not a hazy, hard-to-define concept. It's money. Motivation translates into profits, and that's the bottom line.

Let me give you some hard facts to back that up. A large U.S. retail chain conducted an employee survey to determine the impact of motivation on sales. The difference between how motivated the employees were in the top 25 percent of stores as opposed to the bottom 25 percent amounted to $104 million in sales. The top stores also retained 1,000 more employees per year than did the bottom group of stores.[1] My point: When employees are motivated, turnover decreases and profits increase.

In another study, an accounting firm ran management development centers for 170 high-potential middle managers. These led to significant improvements in motivation, performance, attitude, retention, and job satisfaction. The annual turnover for these managers was 7 percent, compared to 12 percent for the entire management population.[2] Yes, motivation matters. It affects the profitability of the entire organization.

According to numerous studies, well over half of the American workforce lacks motivation.

- 73 percent of employees say they are less motivated today than they used to be.

- 69 percent of operating managers call "lack of employee motivation" the most challenging problem they face in their organization.
- 84 percent of employees say they could perform significantly better if they wanted to.
- 50 percent of employees say they are putting only enough effort into their work to hold on to their jobs.[3]

An employee survey of the U.S. workforce conducted by Gallup found that nearly 20.6 million workers, or 15 percent of employees, are disengaged or fundamentally disconnected from their jobs. The consequences of an unmotivated workforce are lost productivity, absence, illness, and other problems that result when employees are not engaged. Disengaged workers are significantly less productive, less loyal to their companies, more stressed about their jobs, and more insecure about their work than their engaged colleagues.[4] Another Gallup survey found that unmotivated workers are absent from work 3.5 more days a year than other workers—or 86.5 million days for the entire workforce.[5]

These studies highlight just how crucial motivation is in the workplace. The fact is, employee motivation can make or break your business.

Hiring the Motivated and Motivating the Hired

I still make most of the hiring decisions for the key positions in our company. However, I now have a strategic advantage. Because of the research I've done on motivational profiling, I know how to assess both the positions and the people who apply for them. When we have an important spot to fill in our company, I first *profile the position*. I list all

of the non-negotiable aptitudes that we need for the job. Then I cata-
logue the behaviors, skills, and experience that the "ideal candidate"
for the position needs. What qualities and competencies would my
dream employee have that would make him or her perfect for the job?
I write down those attributes. This exercise reveals the Motivational
DNA type that would be best suited for the opening.

For example, if I am hiring a personal assistant I look for a PSI (Pro-
duction-Stability-Internal). Assuming two applicants possess equivalent skills and experience, but one is a PSI and the other is a CVE
(Connection-Variety-External), I will hire the PSI as my assistant.
Why? First, as a Producer myself, I know that I will function better
with an assistant who can match my pace and achievement style.
Second, I realize that the position will not entail a great deal of interaction with others. If I hire a Connector, she is almost certain to become dissatisfied by the solitude of the job. I want a Stabilizer, because
she will work well unsupervised and have the ability to stay on task
until she figures out solutions. Someone who has a need for Variety
would want more diversity than the position entails. Finally, I look
for an Internal, because I want an assistant who lights up when she
plugs into a big vision. I seldom do anything just for money. I am
extremely mission-minded and I need an assistant who thrives on contribution.

Hiring is just one of the many ways that you can use Motivational
DNA in a work setting. In fact, it was the glaring absence of a business
application for motivation that first inspired me to seek one. Sales,
management, finance, customer service, human resources, information technology . . . every other business discipline has precise systems
or professional techniques that can be applied to do the job better.
There are processes and procedures that can be utilized to improve
performance in all of these areas. But there was no step-by-step system
to help businesspeople increase motivation. Now there is. Motivational

DNA fills the void. It will help you in management, marketing, training, development, administration, and much more.

Before we zoom in on the finer points needed to use Motivational DNA with others, it would be valuable to compare and contrast this approach with other motivational theories and profiling tools.

Human motivation is a widely investigated subject and has produced many useful ideas. Educational and social psychologists have constructed a number of concepts, such as drive reduction, affective arousal, cognitive dissonance, and needs theories. I've chosen four of the more popular motivational models to examine here.

ABRAHAM MASLOW
HIERARCHY OF NEEDS

In 1943, behavioral psychologist Abraham Maslow published a paper describing his motivational theory. Maslow's *Hierarchy of Needs* has become widely known and accepted. It was a groundbreaking concept in its day, and an overview of contemporary motivational theory would be incomplete without its inclusion. Maslow contended that as a person's basic needs are met he seeks to satisfy higher needs, ascending up a hierarchy often depicted as a pyramid, built on five levels.

Level 1: Physiological Needs

The lowest level in Maslow's Hierarchy of Needs is made up of Physiological needs—things like breathing, food, water, sleep, and shelter. Maslow said that only when these basic needs are met can a person move up to the next level, Safety.

Level 2: Safety

This level consists of security, health, and well-being needs.

Level 3: Love/Belonging

After Physiological and Safety needs are met, Maslow said a person will try to satisfy his or her need for Love or Belonging. At this level, a person seeks fulfilling friendships, sexual intimacy, and supportive family relationships.

Level 4: Esteem

The next level on Maslow's Hierarchy of Needs is Esteem. This refers to a person's needs for acceptance, respect, and recognition.

Level 5: Self-Actualization

Maslow called the top of the pyramid Self-Actualization, a term he borrowed from his mentor, Kurt Goldstein. In short, Self-Actualization is reaching one's fullest potential. Maslow contended that each need must be satisfied before a person is motivated to move to the next level, and that if at any time one of the lower-level needs is unmet, a person will regress to that level.

DOUGLAS MCGREGOR
THEORY X AND THEORY Y

In the 1960s, social psychologist Douglas McGregor developed the motivational theories known as Theory X and Theory Y. McGregor proposed two schools of thought about employee motivation.

Theory X took a pessimistic view of workers, claiming that people are inherently lazy, lack ambition, want to avoid responsibility, and must be forced to work. Managers who ascribe to Theory X believe that it is their job to push employees to perform. These managers develop an authoritarian style based on the threat of punishment.

Theory Y suggested that employees *may* be motivated to work if given the right conditions. The assumption put forth in Theory Y is that most people want to do well at work and are eager to assume greater responsibilities, but they need to be incentivized. In a nutshell, it's the "carrot-and-stick" theory.

DAVID MCCLELLAND
THREE NEEDS THEORY

About the same time that McGregor was developing Theories X and Y, Harvard psychologist David McClelland was working on what he came to call the *Three Needs Theory*. McClelland hypothesized that workers are motivated by three needs:

1. Affiliation
2. Achievement
3. Authority

McClelland asserted that managers who have a high degree of affiliation tend to be well liked but find it difficult to lead because they do not want to upset or offend anyone. Managers who have a strong desire for achievement were said to put themselves and their own advancement above organizational objectives.

McClelland classified managers inclined toward authority into two groups: those who sought personal power, and those who wanted institutional power. He saw both as good leaders, but the managers who sought personal power inspired loyalty to themselves, while the managers who were more focused on institutional power inspired loyalty to the organization.

FREDERICK HERZBERG
MOTIVATIONAL HYGIENE

The 1960s was a productive decade for motivational theorists. In 1968, behavioral psychologist Frederick Herzberg developed a theory that he called *Motivational Hygiene*. This theory divides motivation into two categories, Intrinsic and Extrinsic. Intrinsic factors relate to the individual, such as responsibility, promotion, and growth. Extrinsic (or hygienic) factors relate to work environment, such as pay, supervision, and company policy. Herzberg felt that intrinsic factors are more powerful motivators than extrinsic factors.

I believe that all of these concepts have merit and yield some useful information. Of course, none of them are without detractors, and I imagine that my findings about Motivational DNA may also provoke some heated debates.

There has never been a motivational theory postulated that was universally accepted. And as much as theorists may like to present their conclusions as indisputable fact, theories are still theories.

My team and I believe that the conclusions we have reached are accurate and compelling. Are they debatable? Absolutely, as they should be! The soul of science is inquiry.

My objective is simply to introduce a valuable system that has proven to motivate individuals and increase the productivity of teams.

Typological Testing

In my coaching practice I use a number of evaluation tools to help my clients. You are probably familiar with some of the principal testing devices on the market. The DiSC profile is an assessment that groups behavioral styles into four categories: Dominance, Influence, Steadiness, and Conscientiousness. DiSC combines these four megatypes to form fifteen metatypes. The Enneagram has nine basic classifications, and the Myers-Briggs Type Indicator segments people into sixteen different classifications. Other typological systems employ thirty-two categories or more, all with their own innumerable subsets. While each stems from different theoretical origins, in many respects there is little distinction between these systems. In fact, they often compete in the marketplace.

While I feel that each of these tools has value, and I recommend that you try them for your own benefit, my chief complaint is that one must become a practitioner in order to use them successfully with other people. They may yield useful insights for the person who takes the test, but the large number of types, complexity of results, and bewildering terminology embodied in these instruments make it virtually impossible for the average person to use them with other people. Unless one invests the time and money to become a certified specialist, the tools are needlessly confusing and the information is difficult to apply.

For example, many people have trouble remembering the distinctions between the terms "Steadiness" and "Conscientiousness" in the DiSC profile. This is further muddled in the Myers-Briggs model, where one must deduce the various nuances of terms like "Sensing," "Feeling," and "Perceiving." These tools are not user-friendly. They are too bloated with superfluous detail to be of much practical value in everyday life.

By contrast, I'm determined to make sure Motivational DNA is easy to understand and use—for yourself and with others. I don't want to treat this like a foreign language. I have deliberately worked incredibly hard to make Motivational DNA easy for you to embrace and use right off the shelf. Unlike the Enneagram, it's not necessary to (and I'm not making this up) "draw a circle and mark nine equidistant points on its circumference. Designate each point by a number from one to nine, with nine at the top, for symmetry and by convention . . ."

Motivational DNA is simple to grasp, quick to learn, and easy to use. The names of the motivational factors are self-descriptive. It is far more effective than any other profiling tool I've ever used. It does not simply give the user a generalized behavioral or personality profile. Instead, it specifically concentrates on the unique combination of factors that motivate, inspire, and mobilize people to meaningful action.

Now let me tell you what this system is not:

1. **It is not a magic pill.** Motivational DNA will not make you taller, stronger, or smarter. You will not necessarily become a world-champion athlete or a Fortune 500 CEO by using the techniques I suggest. Motivational DNA will, however, motivate you to accomplish the things you most want to do. It can inspire you to achieve tough goals and increase your effectiveness. It will also help you to lead and motivate others. It will empower you to empower them.

2. **Motivational DNA is not designed to stereotype or pigeonhole people.** On the contrary, the entire foundation of Motivational DNA rests upon *individuality*. Motivational DNA focuses on our individual uniqueness. The beauty of Motivational DNA is that it identifies your motivational factors and accelerates your achievement. It doesn't say, "This is who you are and who you forever will be," but rather, "This is how you are best motivated and how you can develop even more."

3. **Motivational DNA is not fully automatic.** In order for it to work, you must use it. Information without implementation is

useless. It is not enough for you to understand the principles of Motivational DNA; you have to apply those principles to get results.

The Secret to Motivating, Inspiring, and Energizing Others

At some point in our lives, we have all been inspired by someone else. Perhaps it was a childhood sports coach, an encouraging friend, or a great boss. I had a particularly energetic sixth-grade teacher who acted out the entire Second World War. He used props and sound effects, stood on his desk, threw balls of paper around the room, and fired a water pistol. He entertained and educated his students by bringing history to life. He engaged our adolescent attention in ways that motivated us to learn. I had another teacher who was equally motivating but who used an entirely different approach. She was not an energetic dynamo. Instead, she was soft-spoken. But her highly organized and creative lesson plans kept us energized. She employed activities, illustrations, games, and surprises that made learning an adventure.

Are there secrets to motivating others? Yes, there are. You may have noticed from the examples I just gave about my teachers that those educators appealed to my motivational style—particularly my need for variety. The real key to motivating people and teams is to find out what they love and what they're good at. This is the critical information that sparks motivation. Knowing what people love and where they excel is essential to understanding how to motivate them.

I love music, and although I can sing and play guitar adequately, no one would mistake me for a gifted musician. Even though I enjoy it, I'm not exceptionally good at it. As a result, I lack the motivation to practice. In fact, I haven't picked up my guitar in more than a year. Loving an activity that you don't do well is not enough to sustain your motivation for it over the long haul.

In order to get motivated and stay motivated, a person has to (1) *like the activity* and (2) *be able to do it well.* The chart below provides a visual representation of this truth.

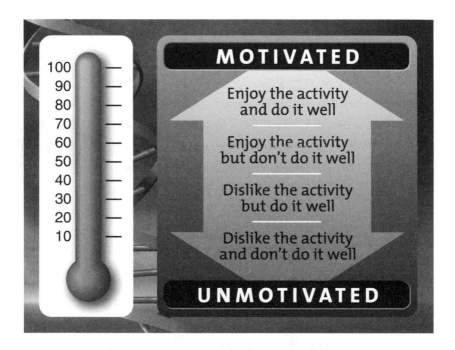

You can measure your degree of enthusiasm for any task or activity based on the criteria listed above. For example, although I dislike mingling with strangers at parties, I happen to be quite good at it. People assume that I enjoy socializing because I do it well. But simply having a natural ability doesn't motivate me to want to do it. I'd still prefer not to mix and mingle at social gatherings, because I don't enjoy it.

So how do you determine the motivational types of the people around you? Is there an easy, accurate way of assessing the motivational preferences of others? Yes, there are actually three ways.

1. **Passive Observation:** If you don't know a person well, or feel uncomfortable asking them questions, look for clues about their motivational type. I'll show you how to do this in just a moment.

2. **Friendly Inquiry:** Ask nonthreatening questions to find out what motivates people. Here are some questions that will help you discover the Motivational DNA of others:
   a. "What kinds of things do you enjoy doing?"
   b. "What activities do you excel at?"
   c. "Which do you like better, structure or spontaneity?"
   d. "Do you prefer to work alone or with others?"
   e. "Are you more competitive or cooperative?"
   f. "What makes you feel most appreciated at work?"
   g. "How do you like to be rewarded for a job well done?"

Remember, this is not an interrogation. You should be carrying on a conversation, not conducting an inquisition.

3. **Active Presentation:** Discuss the Motivational DNA ideas in this book. Most people will be intrigued by the concept and eager to take the profile. Your friends and associates are welcome to go to www.GetMotivatedBook.com to take the free Motivational DNA test. You may also invite them to share their results with you. If they enter your e-mail address at the conclusion of the test, a copy of their profile will be sent to you.

Spotting the Clues

When asked where he got his scientific ideas, Albert Einstein explained that he believed scientific work proceeds best from an examination of physical reality and a search for underlying axioms, with consistent explanations that apply in all instances and avoid contradicting one another. In a nutshell, Einstein looked for clues. He started with what he could see and then dug below the surface to find explanations.

That's precisely how we can identify motivational preferences in others. You don't have to be a weatherman to determine which way the wind is blowing. You can spot clues about a person's Motivational DNA by noting his or her manner of dress, body language, pace, communication style, and environment. For example, Producers often wear power suits. Colorful, flashy clothing, on the other hand, may be a tip-off that you're dealing with someone who is a Variable. Stabilizers generally prefer conservative clothing. Externals tend to be brand conscious.

Pay attention to how people arrange their work environments. Stabilizers are usually neat and organized; Variables may enjoy photos, desk toys, and conversation pieces scattered around their workspace. Connectors encourage visitors, while Producers may discourage people from dropping by to limit interruptions. These kinds of visible indicators reveal clues to a person's motivational traits.

You can also look for what I call "hot buttons." Hot buttons disclose the dominant motivational style a person is operating in at any given time. The chart on the next page shows you how to spot a person's hot buttons so that you know how to motivate him or her.

HOT BUTTONS

Hot Buttons reveal the dominant motivational style
a person is operating in at any given time.

P

If they . . . are speaking fast, are in a hurry, have a commanding presence, are goal-oriented and task-driven, are
interested in leading others or controlling the situation:

Then you relate to them as a Producer.

C

If they . . . have a friendly presence, calm pace, want to
spend time talking, are "touchy-feely," seem loyal, steady,
and dependable:

Then you relate to them as a Connector.

S

If they . . . are concerned about order, schedule, structure, or
rules; are concentrating, focused, studious; seem quiet and
serious:

Then you relate to them as a Stabilizer.

V

If they . . . are animated, expressive, high-energy, are
interested in having fun, think outside the box, are original
and creative, seem to have a short attention span:

Then you relate to them as a Variable.

I

If they . . . want a sense of meaning or significance; are
concerned about philosophical ideals, how decisions will
make a positive difference on the organization or the world;
want to adhere to their strong value system:

Then you relate to them as an Internal.

E

If they . . . are interested in pay, advancement, status, public
recognition, climbing the corporate ladder, gaining
prominence or influence:

Then you relate to them as an External.

Remember, there is a fine line between motivation and manipulation. Our goal with Motivational DNA is always to empower others, not to control them. Motivational DNA allows you to motivate people positively, in the ways they were meant to be motivated. It respects them as individuals. To motivate others, first identify their unique achievement code (their Motivational DNA) and then use compatible motivators to inspire them to action.

Many people have motivational styles that are opposite from your own, and in the past you may have found it challenging to deal with those individuals. So how do you motivate people who have a completely different motivational code from your own? It's one thing to recognize that you have an employee, son, daughter, or boss who has a conflicting motivational code, but how do you deal with it on a practical level? My son Zack, for example, has a motivational style that is very different from my own. How do I handle that?

As I mentioned earlier, when you want to motivate yourself, it is essential that you understand your own motivational type. But when you are motivating someone else, your type is irrelevant. When dealing with others, all that matters is *their* type. You must modify how you interact with them—based on their type, not your own—in order to get the best results. For instance, my son is a Stabilizer but I am a Variable. When I want to motivate Zack, I normally need to deal with him in Stabilizer mode. I must communicate and interact with him as though I were a Stablizer myself. (In a moment, I'll introduce a powerful concept called behavioral cloning that will help you to do this too.)

Earlier I cautioned you not to be overly concerned about memorizing the various combinations of Motivational DNA, but rather to focus on the universally motivating factors of Production, Connection, Stability, Variety, and Internal Awards, and External Awards. Here's why: Even though my son is a Stabilizer, there are settings and situations where his motivational style shifts to one of Variety. At that point, my method of communicating with Zack must also shift. If I continue relating to him as a Stabilizer when he is in Variable mode, there will be a disconnect. To engage his motivation, I need to adapt my behaviors and reestablish connection.

Each of us has a predominant motivational type—the groove that we feel most comfortable in and fall back to again and again. However, in various settings and circumstances, all of us fluctuate between *all six of the universal motivators*. This is why I say that the six factors are more important to understand than the precise way that the factors combine. There is a more advanced method of evaluating Motivational DNA, but it is time-consuming and laborious to use. I worked incredibly hard to make the system in this book easy to use so that you *would* use it—not just stick it up on a shelf.

As with deoxyribonucleic acid (DNA), Motivational DNA can be fairly involved as one goes farther with it. I could teach you how the different types interact with one another and delineate the many distinctions among them, and I intend to post some of that online in the future for those who are interested in the more technical aspects. But the real value of this system is derived from knowing how to recognize the six factors of Motivational DNA and respond to them in daily life.

Behavioral Cloning

I believe that *rapport* is the most irresistible force in business. Rapport is the experience of being in agreement with someone you trust. When a person is in rapport with you, he or she is inclined to concur, cooperate, and collaborate with you. The next concept I am going to discuss, behavioral cloning, will help you to create an environment of agreement that builds rapport.

Cloning is the process of creating an identical copy of something. In biology, it refers to the methods used to produce copies of DNA, cells, or organisms. What I call "behavioral cloning" is the *reproduction of the language, posture, and pacing of another person.* It is a powerful means of establishing trust and understanding with others.

People and teams who work well together generally share similar communication styles, gestures, and behaviors. This is an innate expression of behavioral cloning. We often see this in married couples. After many years of marriage, the body language, communication styles, dress, and behaviors of husbands and wives tend to be strikingly similar. Likewise, people who are in rapport usually demonstrate well-matched communication styles and body language. Effective work teams frequently coin their own "language" (acronyms, inside jokes, and jargon) to describe their common experience.

The next time you are in a restaurant, observe the diners and you'll get a real-time lesson in behavioral cloning. If the tablemates are having a good time, you'll notice that they often share similarities in posture and speech. If one person is leaning forward, all tend to be leaning forward. If one is cross-legged, they are all cross-legged. Their gestures and even their expressions will be alike. Next, take a look at the people who seem uncomfortable or unhappy with their companions. You'll pick up dissimilarities in how they are talking, sitting, and gesturing. There is a disconnect that shows up in their body language and speech patterns. One may speak rapidly in a loud voice, while the other speaks slowly with a lowered tone. One may be carefully focused on her companion, while the other avoids eye contact.

In order to communicate effectively with others, it helps to create a space where people feel understood, appreciated, and safe. The more you are able to bring your communication style and body language into alignment with others, the easier it will be to gain rapport. You may have noticed when speaking with a small child that if you kneel down to their level and make eye contact when you speak, there is a greater sense of connection. The same is true with adults. Behavioral cloning places you on the same level, so to speak, and strengthens the bond.

The next time you want to inspire someone to take action, match their body language, tonality, and pacing. If they are fast-paced, pick up your pace when you speak to them. If they are seated at a table with their hands folded, have a seat and do the same. Conforming your posture and communication style to that of the person you are speaking with can help to create unity by making the other person feel accepted and understood.

As you practice behavioral cloning with others, remember that you are *matching* their style, not mocking them. You don't want to mirror their behavior, just model it. Your voice, gestures, and body language ought to be similar but not identical. Here are the behavioral elements that you want to pay attention to and try to harmonize with:

- ❏ Posture
- ❏ Body language
- ❏ Gestures
- ❏ Facial expressions
- ❏ Eye contact
- ❏ Pitch of voice
- ❏ Tonality
- ❏ Pacing (rhythm and speed)
- ❏ Volume
- ❏ Words and phraseology

Start by cloning just one behavior—for example, how a person is sitting or standing. When you are comfortable with doing that, work on matching vocal patterns. As you practice the skill of behavioral cloning, you'll discover that it not only helps you motivate others, it will enhance your relationships.

How to Motivate and Inspire Groups of People

The techniques I have discussed so far have been focused on individuals. But what you should you do when dealing with more than one person? How can you motivate a classroom of students, or an entire team? In every group of people, you will find an assortment of motivational types and a variety of communication styles. The mistake that many people make is to appeal to the whole group on the basis of their own motivational type. For example, people I refer to as Variables may be enthusiastic and passionate, but if they don't create a logical plan of action and present factual reasons for taking that action, the Stabilizers on the team or in the audience will not be swayed.

To motivate groups, you must appeal to every motivational style. You need to offer something for everyone: interaction for the Connectors, challenge for the Producers, structure for the Stabilizers, diversity for the Variables, and a combination of Internal and External Awards to spur performance.

As we move into Part Two, I will focus on the six universal motivators of Motivational DNA. We will build on your understanding of Motivational DNA as you discover what to do (and what *not* to do) to motivate people of every motivational type. We'll also look at each style and learn about:

- Their strengths and weakness
- What they sound like
- How they think
- How to effectively communicate with them
- How to resolve conflict with them
- How to inspire and lead them
- How they respond at work, at play, and in their relationships

- How they influence others
- Their value to an organization

We'll conclude each chapter of Part Two with suggestions for each type.

A MOTIVATIONAL TIP FOR COUPLES

While reading Part Two, highlight everything that is true about you. Get a second copy of this book for your partner. Invite your partner to highlight the second book to indicate everything that is true about him or her. Then switch books. This is the quickest, easiest, and most effective way to truly understand your mate. You'll learn what makes them feel fulfilled, valued, motivated, and loved.

A MOTIVATIONAL TIP FOR SINGLES

One of the secrets to selecting a compatible mate is deciding exactly what type of person you would like to spend the rest of your life with. As you go through Part Two, highlight the qualities and character attributes that you'd like in a future mate. This will clarify your thinking and give you an unbiased "checklist" for evaluating potential partners.

Now let's learn more about the only six things that motivate everyone: Production, Connection, Stability, Variety, Internal Awards, and External Awards.

FREE BONUS #4
A 60-Minute Webinar with Tamara Lowe,
"On Motivation, Leadership and Teambuilding" Plus
GET MOTIVATED Study Guides for Business Owners,
CEO's, and Managers who want to train their employees
to use Motivational DNA at work. ($229 value)

It really does take teamwork to make the dream work. Join me and my panel of leadership and teambuilding experts for a one-hour webinar that will help you create a motivational climate in your organization and reenergize your entire team.

Special: If you are a business owner, CEO, or manager who would like your employees to read, discuss and implement the Motivational DNA concepts from *Get Motivated!* to increase the performance and profitability of your organization, we are happy to provide you with FREE Study Guides for every member of your team!

PART TWO

THE DNA OF CHAMPIONS

How Producers Produce

"If you lead a country like Britain, a strong country, a country
which has taken a lead in world affairs in good times
and in bad, a country that is always reliable, then you have to have
a touch of iron about you."

—MARGARET THATCHER

L ady Thatcher is the most brilliant and articulate woman I have ever known. She is an expert in law, politics, economics, and world affairs, but what has amazed me is her encyclopedic knowledge about everything—and I do mean *everything*—else. Margaret Thatcher can speak with clarity, insight, and conviction about any topic that is raised. I have yet to see her stumped by any subject.

She understands business better than the billionaire corporate titans I know. No matter how obscure or complex the issue, she is astonishingly well informed and eloquent about it. If the lady is made of iron, that iron is forged in the shape of a vault containing the wealth of knowledge she has amassed.

Margaret Thatcher is a Producer. Educated at Oxford, she studied chemistry and later worked as a research chemist. At twenty-five, she was the youngest female Conservative candidate to ever stand for election to Parliament. At twenty-eight, she became a barrister, specializing in tax law. Later, she entered the Cabinet as Education Secretary. Then, in 1979, Mrs. Thatcher was elected Prime Minister, becoming the first woman ever to take the role. Winning three consecutive elections, she remained the longest-serving Prime Minister in more than 150 years.

Time magazine, which recognized her as one of the most influential people in the world, wrote, "The triumph of capitalism, the almost universal acceptance of the market as indispensable to prosperity, the collapse of Soviet imperialism, the downsizing of the state on nearly every continent and in almost every country in the world—Margaret Thatcher played a part in all those transformations, and it is not easy to see how any would have occurred without her."

But Thatcher became a global icon for more than just her politics. She combined razor-sharp intelligence and ironclad resolve with elegance and femininity. This fascinating fusion kept the world watching and helped engrave her place in history. Like all Producers, Margaret Thatcher is a confident, results-oriented achiever who likes to be in charge. She is a commanding presence. She knows it and so does everyone who flies in her orbit. She once said to me, "Tamara, being powerful is like being a lady. If you have to tell people you are, then you aren't."

Temperament

Producers are natural leaders. Classic "Type A" personalities, they are overachievers with a can-do attitude. Producers are self-assured, bold, and decisive. Wired for leadership, they love to take charge. Producers are authoritative and assertive—go-getters who feel that they can conquer any challenge if given the chance. They possess extraordinary willpower and self-discipline.

Producers can get done in a few hours what might take most people a whole day to do. They are fast, efficient, and competent. Fast-paced and task-oriented, Producers love a challenge and tend to face them head-on. They'll find a way to hurdle any obstacle they encounter.

Quick decision makers, they can be indispensable in times of crisis. They possess the courage to face difficulties and the confidence that they will prevail. In fact, they thrive under pressure. Producers are "fixers"—they have half a dozen solutions for every dilemma. Whatever the problem, Producers believe it can be figured out and solved.

Highly autonomous, Producers seek the freedom to do what they want, when they want, and how they want. They like to have control over their lives, professionally and personally. Self-confident and self-reliant, Producers tend to be extremely independent. Wanting everything to move along, Producers become impatient with problems that linger and people who loiter.

Producers are able to read others well. They are good at assessing people's weaknesses, as well as their strengths. Producers enjoy helping others succeed. They set very high standards for themselves, as well as for those they lead. When others do not perform at the high level expected, Producers are apt to be critical. But their expectations often incite their coworkers to rise to the challenge. Others see Producers as smart and skilled—people who have their act together. At their best, Producers combine efficiency, competence, and inspiring optimism to create positive change.

The Self-Governing Producer

A few years ago, one of my senior managers came to me and expressed frustration about one of his subordinates. Mark stepped into my office and I invited him to take a seat.

"What's on your mind?" I asked.

Let the mudslinging begin. Mark interpreted my question as an invitation to let it fly.

"It's Charlie," Mark said. "He's driving me crazy. He is incredibly difficult to work with. He's always rubbing people the wrong way. He acts like the end justifies the means. Charlie thinks he can make up his own rules. He's like a bulldozer. He just plows over people."

And then the inevitable conclusion—the one I knew was coming. . . . Mark took a deep breath and said, "I can't work with him anymore. I want to let Charlie go."

"Of course you do," I said. "But can you tell me about his good qualities?"

Reluctantly, as if I'd asked him to donate a kidney, Mark said, "Well, I admit Charlie is a hard worker. He comes in early; he stays late. He's smart and he's fast. And he's a high achiever. He's like a dependable running back that you pass the ball to when you're third and long. You know he'll make the play—but he will crush anyone who gets in his way. He'll get the first down, but there will be bodies from both teams all over the field."

"Promote him," I said.

"Promote him? I don't want to promote him! I want to fire him!"

"I know," I said. "But the problem with Charlie is that you have him doing the job of a follower, when he is clearly a leader. The guy is stepping all over people because he's too big for the position. Promote him and give him some freedom. Let's see how he does."

So we promoted Charlie and he absolutely flourished. Within a few years, he was a senior executive in our company. Producers need autonomy. Their manner can appear unconventional and even unreasonable, but there is a method to the mayhem.

Recently, my husband, Peter (a classic Producer), had a dictation system installed so that he could phone his assistant and leave her detailed voice mails that she could later transcribe. The first message that was put on the machine simply said, "You may begin recording now."

"I need to call this line dozens of times each day," Peter said to the technician installing the machine. "I don't have time to listen to that message. It's too long. Could you please shorten it?"

The technician was taken aback. How could he shorten a five-word message? He agreed to try and recorded this instead: "Begin recording now."

"That's better, but it's still too long," Peter said. "Can you get it down to one word?"

"Impossible!" said the tech.

"No, that's not going to work," Peter said. "It doesn't make sense. Plus it's too long. Four syllables."

"I wasn't talking about the word—I was talking about the concept," the tech said.

Ignoring the so-called impossible concept, Peter exclaimed, "GO! That's the word. Please record the word GO!"

Now when Peter phones his recording system, he gets one ring, hears the word "GO!" and has instant access to the dictation device. That makes my husband, the Producer, very happy. He's free to control the universe without all those annoying syllables to slow him down.

PRODUCERS IN THEIR OWN WORDS

*"I have a tendency to go through my life at full speed and as a
one-man band, so I don't generally stop and take in other people
enough to develop many relationships."*
—Gillian Anderson

"Control your own destiny or someone else will."
—Jack Welch

"When you confront a problem, you begin to solve it."
—Rudolph Giuliani

*"As one goes through life, one learns that if you don't
paddle your own canoe you don't move."*
—Katharine Hepburn

"An ounce of action is worth a ton of theory."
—Friedrich Engels

"A perpetual holiday is a good working definition of hell."
—George Bernard Shaw

*"My philosophy of life is that if we make up our mind what
we are going to make of our lives, then work hard toward that goal,
we never lose—somehow we win out."*
—Ronald Reagan

"A team effort is a lot of people doing what I say."
—Michael Winner, director and producer

*"Success is almost totally dependent upon drive and persistence.
The extra energy required to make another effort or
try another approach is the secret of winning."*
—Denis Waitley

*"They always say time changes things, but you actually
have to change them yourself."*
—Andy Warhol

*"Effective leadership is not about making speeches or being liked;
leadership is defined by results."*
—Peter Drucker

Communication Style

Producers are straightforward and direct. They tend to be fast-paced in their communications and dislike repeating themselves; they hate spending a lot of time explaining. They expect others to just "get it." Producers like to get to the point quickly and want others to do the same. Because of that, some people may see them as tactless. But Producers just like people to say what's on their mind rather than mince words or sidestep the issues.

Producers do not tend to be great listeners. They are more task-oriented than people-oriented and prefer to focus on the job at hand. Listening to others is seen as a waste of time, because the Producer often believes he already knows the question and has the answer.

Consequently, Producers can come across as hurried and impatient. They generally find small talk and chitchat tedious. Others are sometimes offended by their frankness. In the movie *A Beautiful Mind*, Russell Crowe's character, John Nash, explains it this way: "I find that polishing my interactions in order to make them sociable requires a tremendous effort. I have a tendency to expedite information flow by being direct. Often I don't get a good result."

When Communicating with Producers
- ❏ Edit your thoughts before speaking. Try not to be overly talkative.
- ❏ Be concise. Communicate information as succinctly as possible.
- ❏ The faster you can spit it out, the more they'll appreciate it.
- ❏ Get to the point and don't worry about being too direct—Producers can handle it.

Cognitive Process

Producers are "big picture" thinkers. They look beyond the present chaos and see future possibilities. Producers think about the consecutive steps needed to achieve a goal, mentally charting their entire course from start to finish. They are able to consider the variables and make a swift determination whether a proposed solution is going to work or not. They take calculated risks, and because of their foresight and intuition, those choices usually play out in their favor. With a talent for long-range thinking, Producers focus on getting the best results as efficiently and quickly as possible.

Producers prefer a self-directed learning style. They want to know the "what" and work to figure out the "how, when, and why" by themselves. Producers like data to be presented in a concise, structured format. They are generally fast learners and are able to process new information rapidly.

Quick on their feet, Producers tend to rely on themselves to come up with the answers to problems. They often make decisions without checking with others for input. When they make a choice they believe is right, Producers don't feel a need for approval from others. They are deliberate decision makers and their gut instincts tend to be right.

Producers show better judgment than many people, especially in high-pressure situations. It's difficult for them to just stand back and let events unfold. Producers need either to be in control or to feel that the situation is under control. Easily irritated by lack of follow-through, when they ask for something to be done, they expect it to get done.

Typically optimistic, Producers believe that everything is possible if they set their mind to it. As far as Producers are concerned, success is not a matter of chance but a matter of choice. The possibility of failure doesn't enter into most Producers' minds. They believe that they can influence or manage most of the things that happen in their lives. Their motto is: "If it's going to be, it's up to me." For better or worse, they are the designers of their destiny.

Likely Strengths

❏ Strong leadership capabilities
❏ Hardworking with the ability to take initiative
❏ Confident and self-assured
❏ Knack for recognizing hidden potential in others
❏ Attacks problems with pit bull resolve
❏ Organized and able to manage multiple projects simultaneously
❏ Excels under pressure
❏ Responds quickly in times of crisis

Possible Pitfalls

Producers are highly competitive and can be domineering in their attempt to achieve results. Sometimes perceived as control freaks, they can be impatient, demanding, and headstrong. Often unaware of how their behavior negatively affects others, Producers may be autocratic, imposing their own agenda and bulldozing dissenters. Outspoken and opinionated, they can be bossy and overbearing.

Producers admire strength in others but disdain weakness. They are aware of their own giftedness and may be egocentric. If someone less competent is put in charge, Producers tend to become exasperated and fault-finding. They can be tactless or even downright rude. Their blunt, abrasive communication style can alienate those who work with them. Agitated by too slow a pace, they can be critical of people they see as methodical and plodding, or people who are long-winded and slow to get to the point.

Producers at Work

If you want to get something done, give it to a Producer. They can juggle and coordinate multiple projects without breaking a sweat. Producers enjoy the exhilaration of living life on the edge, conquering challenges, and achieving extraordinary results. They take stress in stride and are usually unflappable in times of trouble. Producers exhibit the necessary strength and assurance to guide others into new territory, marshaling resources and mobilizing people toward organizational goals. They are gung-ho leaders who have the ability to craft a vision and get people moving toward it, providing strategic guidance along the way.

Producers tend to be workaholics. They are good at organizing and directing. They take swift action to get things done and then move on to the next project. They avoid passing the buck and are able to administrate, manage, and lead. Incompetence irritates them. If you do a good job, they respect you. Do a poor job and they find it intolerable.

Producers tend to work all the angles, overcoming obstacles and executing in accordance with their plans. They take pride in their ability to do many things at once. Producers enlist others to help carry out their ideas because they want to get started implementing the next idea. Producers can delegate in their sleep, but will do things themselves if they think they can do it better or faster.

Nothing is more satisfying to a Producer than realizing progress toward goals and achieving tangible results. Producers are anxious to eliminate waste, organizational inefficiency, and any processes or people that hinder production. They look for ways to do things better, faster, and more economically. Producers also make a habit of reassessing their own performance and finding ways to improve.

Producers want the freedom to make decisions about how they will do their job. They like to figure out what needs to be done and then be left alone to do it. When working with a team, Producers can be overly independent and may override the group. Their chief concern is results. They like having a plan and making things happen. Producers want to have enough authority to ensure that the job gets done properly and on schedule. They prefer to work with clear-thinking, motivated, action-oriented people like themselves. They also expect their organization to have a good strategic plan, as they believe it is a sign of solid, committed leadership.

When Working with Producers

- ❏ Give them the freedom to choose their own projects and teams.
- ❏ Raise the bar—Producers thrive on challenge.
- ❏ Forget micromanaging them—they can manage themselves.
- ❏ Let them have input into their work-related goals and the ability to decide how to achieve them.
- ❏ As much as possible, get out of their way. Producers are extremely independent and need space to do their thing.
- ❏ Don't saddle them with sluggish team members or bureaucratic procedures. It takes the wind out of their sails.
- ❏ Show appreciation for their abilities. Producers need to know that they are respected.

Producers at Play

Producers have a drive for self-mastery. They have an improvement plan for everything—including themselves. Personal growth is a big part of their recreational activities. They excel at competitive sports and enjoy pursuits that keep them moving. Producers often have difficulty unwinding or sitting still, even at home. They feel best when they accomplish a lot. Generally, Producers do not want to spend their leisure time resting. When they "rest" they like to do it in conjunction with something else: going to a movie, golfing, sailing, camping, hiking, or working out. Producers want to see, do, experience, and be involved in everything. Energetic and impatient when things move too slowly, Producers need to go, go, go.

Producers in Relationships

Producers do not have a high need for affiliation—for relationships. They like people but may find too much personal interaction fatiguing. Producers tend to be guarded, avoiding anything too personal. Having limited time for relationships, they handpick the people they surround themselves with and may not have a lot of deep friendships. Producers can be perceived as detached or aloof, with a tendency to underemphasize relationships. They play their cards close to the vest and may cover up deep feelings.

Producers are good providers and are attentive to their family's financial security and well-being. In high-stress situations, many mistake the Producer's achievement drive for an absence of caring. Although they appear tough on the outside, with those they trust, Producers can be very responsive and caring. After work is over, Producers can be fun, celebratory, and entertaining. They enjoy a variety of recreational activities with family and friends.

Resolving Conflict

Producers don't mind tackling conflict. This is an advantage when dealing with disputes. They will not avoid discussing issues that need to be resolved. However, Producers have a strong penchant to believe that they are right. When confronted they may become defensive, stubborn, or hot-tempered, insisting that their way is the best way.

Others would be wise to not lock horns with Producers in a public setting. Deal with Producers privately. If you are able to first own up to your own mistakes and misjudgments, it will often soften a Producer's reaction so that they can acknowledge theirs. Let them blow off steam, then reason with them, pointing out all the areas where they are right or have been successful. Help them preserve their ego. Make sure that the issue at hand doesn't become personal. Present it as a challenge that needs to be conquered. Producers like to fix problems; that's the way they are wired.

How Producers Influence Others

Producers influence others by getting things done, rallying participants, overcoming obstacles, resolving conflicts, refusing to accept defeat, and following through until the task is complete.

Value to Organization

Producers excel at using time and resources efficiently to achieve results. They exhibit strong leadership capabilities and require minimal supervision. Producers can be entrusted with great responsibilities and perform well under pressure. They are able to organize others to move projects forward. Producers have a great deal of energy and stamina, and are determined to achieve their goals.

De-Motivators

You may think Producers are naturally self-motivated. Not so. Like all of the motivational types, in the right environment they are motivated. When Producers have independence and can be in control of their surroundings, they are motivated. But put them in a restrictive setting laden with inefficiency, give them a droning and monotonous job to do, restrict their freedom, burden them with an incompetent supervisor, a slow-paced, uninspiring environment, constant nonessential interruptions, red tape, and little opportunity for advancement—and watch how unmotivated they can become!

Top Ten Motivators

1. Autonomy
2. Freedom to develop and implement ideas
3. Crises, deadlines, or difficult situations to solve
4. Achieving the "impossible"
5. Doing more, doing it better, doing it faster, and breaking records
6. Challenges and contests
7. Working simultaneously on multiple projects
8. Peer respect and recognition by superiors
9. The belief that nobody else can do it better
10. Acknowledgment from others that no one else can do it better

Advice for Producers

Practice deferring to others. Try not to be a bulldozer. Endeavor to relinquish control when you are able to. Learn how to let others lead—

even if they fail. Be careful not to drive people as hard as you drive yourself. Force yourself to slow down, then reach out to and connect with those who are more social than you. Stretch yourself to become more focused on relationships. Listen to and attempt to appreciate other people's points of view. Leadership comes naturally to you, but refrain from the temptation to tell others what they should do and how they should do it. Learn ways to control your annoyance when you are impatient. Slow down. Breathe. Remember that you are a human "being," not a human "doing." Relax. Enjoy life.

FREE BONUS #5
From Tamara's Personal Archive of Celebrity Interviews—
"Principles for Leading Radical Change" by
Mikhail Gorbachev. (Priceless value)

This former president of the Soviet Union and Nobel Peace Prize winner is one of the towering figures of history. He literally changed the world as we know it. In this revealing and compelling article, Mikhail Gorbachev recounts how he set about to change a nation through his dream of democracy and freedom.

The Relationship Secrets
of Connectors

**"No one gets the satisfaction or the joy that I get
out of seeing kids realize there is hope."**
—JERRY LEWIS

Jerry Lewis has been entertaining the world since he was five years old, when he made his stage debut singing "Brother, Can You Spare a Dime?" on New York's Borscht Circuit. By the time he was fifteen, he was performing with veteran comedians. A world-renowned star of stage, screen, and television, Jerry Lewis has a distinctive personality and sense of humor that have made him the King of Comedy. He is a dear man with a huge heart who has single-handedly raised more than two billion dollars to fight muscular dystrophy.

What is the secret of Jerry's success? What motivates him? It can be summed up in one word: people. Jerry has an ongoing love affair with humanity. I've never met anyone who finds relationships as rewarding as Jerry Lewis. He is the ultimate Connector.

I first met Jerry in 2002 when I invited him to speak at one of my

GET MOTIVATED Seminars. Jerry has suffered a number of health problems over the years, and at the time he was confined to a wheelchair. Although he was not feeling well, he was determined to perform "in the round" for our live audience. As he took the stage, more than 15,000 people rose to give him a standing ovation. For forty-five minutes the crowd howled with laughter as he unleashed one joke after another. Afterward, as I chatted with him backstage, I could tell that he was deeply moved by the experience.

"Tamara," he told me, "you have no idea what that just did for me. What an amazing experience! To hear the laughter surrounding me . . . coming from all sides . . . it was 360 degrees of pure joy! It made me so happy to make them happy." With tears in his eyes, he said, "I'd like to do this again. I hope you'll invite me back." Of course, I did—many, many times. I was honored to do so.

Over the next few months, I watched Jerry experience a physical transformation, one that can only be described as miraculous. He lost more than seventy pounds and his health dramatically improved. The doctors were flabbergasted. They had no explanation for it. What's more, *Jerry got out of his wheelchair!* What a wonderful day it was for me when I saw him walk to the stage for the first time, climb the stairs, and stand to perform for more than an hour.

Jerry told me that our GET MOTIVATED audiences literally saved his life. "I don't think I would be here today if it were not for these people. The chance to hear their laughter one more time is what keeps me going. It has added years to my life."

Temperament

Like Jerry Lewis, Connectors are relationship-builders. They seek to develop lasting associations with friends, family, neighbors, and coworkers. Connectors are loyal, empathetic, and supportive. They promote harmony. Warmhearted and well-meaning, they are responsive to the needs of others. Connectors find personal satisfaction in making others happy.

In general, Connectors would rather fit in than stand out. Their need to assimilate keeps them from straying too far from cultural norms. They let time-honored standards and expectations guide them. Connectors are team players. They are inclined to be compassionate and collaborative, honoring the talents of others and seeking to involve everyone.

Connectors are generous with their time but can be *too* compliant, putting their needs on hold to meet the needs of others. Connectors make others feel understood; they make an effort to see other people's point of view. Above all, they look for strong, emotionally satisfying relationships.

The People-Loving Connector

I was just twenty-four years old when I met the father of Positive Thinking, Dr. Norman Vincent Peale. For those of you too young to remember, Dr. Peale was one of America's greatest motivators. His bestselling book *The Power of Positive Thinking*, first published in 1952, sold more than seven million copies and stayed on the *New York Times* bestseller list for an astonishing 186 consecutive weeks. Dr. Peale was also a popular public speaker who served for fifty-three years as the pastor of Marble Collegiate Church in Manhattan. During that time, the church's membership grew to more than 5,000 and he became one of New York City's most famous preachers.

We had the joy and privilege of having Dr. Peale speak for us on his ninetieth birthday. He spoke with the exuberance of a man half his age; we were all astounded by his energy. Afterward, he and his wife, Ruth, stood for more than an hour to greet the attendees, answer questions, autograph books, and pose for photos.

Later, over dinner, I asked Mrs. Peale, "What do you do when there is a long line of people waiting to talk to you and someone steps up, oblivious to the crowd behind them, and begins to tell you their entire life story in exhausting detail?"

Mrs. Peale laughed. "Here's what I do: I hand them a business card with my mailing address on it and I say, 'My dear, that sounds fascinating! Would you please do me a favor? Write all of this down in a letter and mail it to me. I would like to have your story in writing. Here is my personal mailing address. I look forward to receiving your letter!'"

That evening, I passed along Mrs. Peale's wisdom to my husband. A few nights later, following a seminar in Boston, Peter returned to our hotel room looking dog-tired.

I said, "Honey, are you okay? You look beat! What happened?"

"Well, the seminar was fine. Actually, it was a lot of fun," he said. "But afterward, in the hallway, I was accosted by a woman who insisted on telling me every problem she had ever experienced from early childhood until this present moment!"

I laughed. "You should have used the advice Ruth Peale gave me."

"Oh, I did!" Peter said. "I told her, 'My dear, that sounds fascinating! Would you please do me a favor? Write all of this down in a letter, and mail it to Mrs. Peale!'"

CONNECTORS IN THEIR OWN WORDS

*"Cherish your human connections—your relationships
with friends and family."*
—Barbara Bush

"Alone we can do so little; together we can do so much."
—Helen Keller

"I have a fear of being disliked, even by people I dislike."
—Oprah Winfrey

*"Personal relationships are the fertile soil from which
all advancement . . . all success . . . all achievement
in real life grows."*
—Ben Stein

"I can live for two months on a good compliment."
—Mark Twain

"The secret of my success? I am basically a nice person."
—Ron Howard

*"Every student has come to see me in my office at least once.
I cannot teach bodies. I can only relate to people. And so I say,
'Come in, and we will sit across from one another.
I don't want to talk about the texts or the class. We can do that
another time. . . . And when you come, I am going to touch you—
and if that bothers you, take your tranquilizer.' It is amazing
how many are intimidated by someone who says, 'I want to
touch you.' I was raised in a large Italian family, as most of
you know, and everybody hugs everybody all the time."*
—Leo Buscaglia

*"No matter what you do, no matter what you achieve, no matter
how much success you have, no matter how much money you have,
relationships are still the most important."*
—Ed Bradley

"The happiest times in my life were when my relationships
were going well—when I was in love with someone and
someone was loving me."
—Billy Joel

Communication Style

Connectors communicate with warmth. They prefer to relate through personal exchanges, rather than e-mail, fax, or phone. Connectors are open and candid and expect others to be unguarded as well. Considerate gestures, time with others, and mutual support are all essential to their sense of well-being.

Connectors are peacemakers and don't like to rock the boat. They don't want to upset, slight, or snub others. They may skirt the issues to avoid conflict. When people are at odds, Connectors want to help reconcile them.

Connectors have a talent for hearing what's not being said and communicating unexpressed meanings. Because of this they find it unfathomable when others don't understand them, even if they are not conveying their feelings vocally. Nevertheless, Connectors desire to keep things agreeable and will defer to others most of the time. They usually have a hard time sticking up for themselves and may have difficulty expressing the value of their viewpoint.

When Communicating with Connectors

❏ Slow down your pace, soften your tone, and make eye contact.
❏ Don't immediately get down to business—take time for niceties.
❏ Be warm and friendly—Connectors don't like standoffishness.
❏ Give Connectors time to finish their sentences.
❏ Allow them to explain their position without interrupting.

❏ Reach out and touch their arm when making a point. Friendly, non-threatening contact is a bonding element for Connectors.

Cognitive Process

Connectors have an inclusive way of thinking. They see the big picture, particularly how ideas and events affect everyone, not just themselves. Connectors respond to issues with their hearts as well as their heads. They are offended when people are impersonal or insensitive and can become weighed down by other people's problems. Sometimes they feel like they care too much.

In making decisions, they prefer a collaborative approach that takes into account the input and involvement of others. They make decisions in consultation with as many of the players as possible. Connectors incorporate information from many sources and weave together a cohesive picture. They prefer an exploratory approach where information is openly shared and problems are solved as a group.

Connectors prefer to work with others when assimilating new information. They like to get personal direction and positive feedback on how they are doing. Connectors tend to be tactile and visual learners. They like hands-on training, learning activities, and role-playing. They prefer pictures and demonstrations when learning or explaining concepts to others.

Connectors enjoy heart-to-heart exchanges and friendly interactions. They believe that people are the most important part of life. They try very hard to meet expectations and are hard on themselves when they feel like they've failed to measure up. Connectors are intuitive and tend to let their feelings guide them. They can have difficulty with making hard decisions and generally shy away from high-risk situations.

Likely Strengths

❏ Talent for empathetic listening

❏ Good with customer service

❏ Ability to bridge differences and unite people

❏ Dependability: You can count on Connectors when you need them

❏ Very patient and tolerant

❏ Friendly, approachable, and unassuming

❏ Always willing to help

Possible Pitfalls

Connectors can be too trusting, too eager to please, and too slow to address problems for fear of offending or hurting others. They have a difficult time saying no, and will often overload themselves with responsibilities that they neither want nor need to do. Connectors are prone to self-doubt and insecurity. They often have trouble acknowledging their own needs and standing up for themselves.

Sometimes self-conscious and unassertive, Connectors may need supervision to stay on track. They are reluctant to act without guidelines. Flustered by a fast pace, Connectors can get distracted and forget priorities. When inundated with projects, they can feel overwhelmed by deadlines. They may lack focus or freeze up in unexpected situations.

Connectors fear dissent and the disapproval of others, and can be overly tolerant. Their inclination to quietly support and encourage others can lead them to be too pliable.

Connectors at Work

Connectors love having people around—it energizes them. They prefer to work in groups and expect their coworkers to be friendly and respectful. Connectors want to enjoy the company of colleagues and work in a "family" environment. They want to have friends at work.

With their characteristic "we're all in this together" mentality, Connectors are always happy to pitch in and help. They invest themselves in group objectives, often volunteering for the unpleasant chores that others shun. Connectors prefer to do the work themselves rather than delegate, because they don't want to impose on their coworkers. Frequently overextended in their desire to help everyone and meet every need, Connectors can easily become overcommitted and tackle too much.

Connectors strive to consider everyone's ideas, regardless of position, rank, or status. They believe everyone should have a chance to contribute. Even when not working in a group, Connectors feel most at home in a cooperative, collaborative environment. They want to discuss challenges, concepts, and issues with others to better understand the information and determine the solutions.

Because they are open with their time and talents, Connectors expect team members to be willing to share their knowledge and skill with one another. While they quietly encourage the involvement of everyone, the Connectors' own contributions may go unrecognized because they do their work without claiming credit and without fanfare.

As team players, Connectors usually prefer to let others take the lead. It is important to them to have a supervisor whom they like and trust. In a leadership role, Connectors focus on the needs of followers. Connectors desire to have an open give-and-take exchange with their colleagues. They believe that group interaction and mutual consideration are essential to a successful workplace.

When Working with Connectors

❏ Provide them with a clear vision along with a way to measure whether or not they are achieving organizational goals.

❏ Give specific directions and demonstrate exactly how to do new work.

❏ Provide guidance along with ongoing support.

❏ Make sure the Connector knows the lines of authority and whom to go to if there is a problem.

❏ Never isolate Connectors—they will become unhappy and lose motivation.

Connectors at Play

Connectors prefer to spend their free time with other people. Pitching in to help out family and friends is fun for them. They enjoy the simple things in life: nature, a good meal, sports, family life, and friends. They love parties, celebration, and social gatherings. While undeniably friendly and sociable, Connectors are not necessarily the life of the party. They just enjoy being around others. Connectors need contact, anything that brings about an emotional connection.

Connectors in Relationships

Connectors value their ability to network and forge meaningful partnerships and relationships with others. They care about the needs of others and receive satisfaction from helping people. They love being a part of community activities and seek opportunities to interact and grow together.

Maintaining traditions with family, friends, and institutions is important to them. Traditions provide a sense of community and belonging, as well as the continuity they desire.

Sensitive and sometimes insecure, Connectors need to be liked and respected. They desire reassurance, affection, words of appreciation, and love expressed through visible gestures.

Connectors invest a lot in their relationships and can sometimes unwittingly establish a benchmark that others may not be able to meet. Remove their family, work, and community roles and you eliminate their source of happiness.

Resolving Conflict

It takes a lot to truly upset Connectors—and even then, they get over it quickly. Connectors are very accommodating unless they are treated badly or feel taken advantage of. They can lose themselves in relationships, giving and doing to the point where they feel somewhat used. When they get upset, Connectors generally become very quiet. Others may not be aware when Connectors are displeased, because they tend to keep their feelings inside without becoming visibly angered.

When an issue involves conflict, Connectors usually try to steer clear of it rather than doing what is necessary to resolve the problem. With their tendency toward pacification, Connectors would rather put a Band-Aid on a wound than provoke the pain of cleaning it out. They hate confrontation and are inclined to avoid it at all costs, because they don't want to start an argument.

Connectors want relationships to be pleasurable with little tension. They tend to yield rather than wrangle with combustible personalities. When bickering breaks out, they want to reconcile quickly. It distresses them when someone who is quarreling with them tries to walk away. When others speak to them in a confrontational manner, their natural inclination is to withdraw, but their desire to restore harmony forces them to work through the conflict.

How Connectors Influence Others

Connectors get everyone involved to participate. They want everyone to be included and play a part. They influence the group by building camaraderie and proposing equitable solutions.

Value to Organization

Connectors are great team players; they are supportive and helpful. They are the worker bees of any organization, faithfully carrying out their responsibilities. If something needs to be done, they'll do it. They are happy to take on assignments that others don't want if they feel that it is for the good of the team.

Connectors support the group's goals and will pitch in to help wherever needed, shoring up coworkers and assisting them to do their work. They celebrate the success of their team members. Seeking to provide value to the organization and others, Connectors are willing to go to great lengths to help out.

Compassionate and sensitive, Connectors are slow to anger and forbearing with others' flaws. They are very good, empathetic listeners. People open up to them easily. Connectors provide a sounding board for others.

Connectors seek to understand and fulfill the wants and needs of other people. If they know what their leaders expect of them, they will bend over backward to live up to those expectations. Openhanded and bighearted, Connectors are generous to a fault. Unsung heroes, Connectors work hard to achieve team goals while giving others the credit.

De-Motivators

Conflict and isolation are the deadly duo for Connectors. Either one will suck the motivation right out of them.

Top Ten Motivators

1. Quality time with family and friends
2. Sincere compliments and encouragement
3. A work environment that allows socialization
4. Being wanted and needed
5. Harmony
6. Meeting the needs of others
7. Low stress
8. Leisurely pace and open-ended time frames
9. Group activities and decision making
10. Time to talk and bond

Advice for Connectors

Give yourself permission to go at your own pace, but develop the behavioral flexibility to speed up when dealing with people who have a faster tempo. Learn how to say no. Don't be a pushover. People will still like you even when you stand up for yourself. Assertiveness is a virtue, not a flaw.

FREE BONUS #6
**Learn how to expand your sphere of influence with
"Proven Networking Strategies," a 16-page special report.
($39 value)**

Your net worth is directly tied to your network. Learn how to expand your network, and utilize it much more effectively, in this exclusive special report.

Developing the Laser-Sharp Focus of Stabilizers

**"Don't bother people for help without first trying to
solve the problem yourself."**
—GENERAL COLIN POWELL

R ight this way, General," I said as I led Colin Powell down the
hall to where the others had already assembled.

Secretary of State Colin Powell was the guest of honor at
a private dinner that I was hosting. As the General and I made our way
to the dining room, my mother stopped us.

"Mr. Secretary," she said. "May I please take a quick picture of you
and my daughter together?"

"Absolutely," General Powell said. "I'd love to."

The photographer was in the grand salon with the other guests, but
he'd left one of his cameras set up on a tripod. Colin brought me over
to the backdrop, put his arm around me, and smiled. My mom fiddled
with the camera while Colin Powell and I waited.

"I'm not quite sure how this thing works," she said as she pressed various buttons on the camera.

The General and I stood patiently for half a minute. I finally made a move to assist my mother, who was still fumbling with the camera.

"I'll help her," I said.

Colin tightened his grip around me and said in a low voice, "No, let her figure it out. She can do it."

We waited another minute, but sure enough, my mother found the shutter release and took this picture. Whenever I see the snapshot she took, I remember the lesson Colin Powell taught me. It is one of the reasons he is such an inspiring leader: He empowers others.

Portrait of a Stabilizer

A poor boy from the Bronx, New York, Colin Powell rose to become one of America's chief statesmen and one of the most distinguished leaders of the twenty-first century. He spent thirty-five years in the U.S. Army and rose to the rank of four-star general. He served as Chairman of the Joint Chiefs of Staff, was a key aide to the Secretary of Defense, and became President Ronald Reagan's National Security Advisor. In 2001, newly elected President George W. Bush appointed Colin Powell to serve as Secretary of State, making him the first African American to hold this office.

I've had the pleasure of working with General Powell for more than twenty years and have observed up close the extraordinary talents of this remarkable man. As a leader, General Powell is a Stabilizer first and foremost, and that's what makes him so good at what he does. But he is one of those rare achievers who score high in all six of the motivational factors. It is neither exaggeration nor idolization to say that General Powell is a genius. It is quite simply a fact.

Consistent, steady, reliable, smart, controlled, and prepared: These are characteristics of a strong Stabilizer, and General Powell is the personification of these traits. Yet he recognizes that change is part of life and has mastered the behavioral flexibility to deal with it skillfully.

General Powell is an exceptional communicator—a talent that is normally more closely associated with Variables. And, like all Variables, he has a fun-loving, playful side. A few years ago, the General had a foot injury and had to use a little scooter to get around. He put a trumpet horn on the handlebars and had a grand time honking at people as he zoomed through the backstage corridors at our seminars.

As for his motivational drive, General Powell is a Producer, yet he also has the ability to connect with people like few others. I've seen him personally greet thousands of soldiers. He has often shaken hands, exchanged words, and taken photographs for hours on end with hundreds of military men and women.

General Powell has an Internal Award system, but he also values External Awards. He appreciates the privileges that his positions have afforded him, but his main motivation is to make a mark on the world—and that he most certainly has. The motivational dexterity that Colin Powell displays is part of the reason that he has succeeded in such an outstanding fashion and has become one of the most admired people in the world.

Temperament

Stabilizers like routine, organization, systems, and structure. While others may try to assemble something they know nothing about by guesswork, Stabilizers would rather read the manual and do it right the first time. Dependable, practical, and sensible, Stabilizers are disciplined workers who like uninterrupted time to focus. They are loyal in their friendships, at work, and with family.

Fools rush in where Stabilizers fear to tread. The goal of the Stabilizer is to eliminate the unexpected and prepare for every contingency. They want to plan ahead so that they are not caught off guard by possible problems. They like predictability and knowing that things will go as expected. Stabilizers are naturally resistant to change, especially sudden change.

Stabilizers are good at seeing patterns and have a natural ability to pick up on inconsistencies. They see the holes, flaws, pitfalls, and problems—and are quick to point them out. Careful and cautious, Stabilizers have a penchant for precision. Some people may think they are hairsplitting at times, but Stabilizers see the value of being exact. They appreciate accuracy and attention to detail.

Highly organized, Stabilizers generally prepare a list of things to do every day, and they don't understand how others can operate without a daily written plan. They enjoy creating order from bedlam. Stabilizers are usually doers, not dreamers. However, when they dream, they have a capacity for the kind of in-depth deliberation and persistence that can translate dreams into reality.

Responsible, conscientious, and diligent, Stabilizers have a great deal of self-control. They are moderate and disciplined in their approach to spending and saving. Financially conservative, they feel comfortable operating within a framework of budgets.

Stabilizers tend to be private and shun too much attention. They generally expect a lot of themselves and are harder on themselves than others are on them. A sense of equity is extremely important to them. Stabilizers believe in fairness and justice for all. They cannot just stand by idly and watch people do things wrong.

Stabilizers don't buy into new things easily. They have to make sense, be tested, and be fully operational. Stabilizers are cautious. Before they act, they weigh the probable costs and consequences.

The Studious Stabilizer

One of my life goals (#53, to be exact) was to beat my four-year-old chess champion at his own game. Unfortunately, he's fifteen now and I haven't defeated him. Yet.

My firstborn son is a Stabilizer. When he was four years old, he asked me to teach him how to play chess. He had seen a chess competition at a local bookstore and wanted to learn how the pieces moved. I didn't think he was old enough to understand the game, but he insisted that I show him. Of course, all parents are inclined to think that their children are prodigies, but my husband and I were astonished when Zack picked up the game right away. That afternoon, Peter went out and bought our preschooler a computer chess program. Zack spent three hours playing chess on the computer that day. Before long, we were attending chess tournaments every weekend and Zack was racking up trophy after trophy.

Chess is a game that requires you to think several moves ahead. Stabilizers are good at this. I am a Variable and, regrettably, I don't have the innate talent or patience to do that. I remember playing chess with Zack one day when he was about six years old; he never tired of beating me.

"I'm setting a trap," he said. "Don't you see that?"

"No."

"Why can't you see that, Mom? I've done the same thing for the past three games. I'll set you up to take my pawn with your bishop, and then I'll move my rook. You'll take my bishop with your queen, but then I'll capture your queen with my knight. Do you see it now?"

"I lost you at 'I'm setting a trap.'"

The child sighed. "I'm going to have you in checkmate in four moves."

STABILIZERS IN THEIR OWN WORDS

"I was born in Harlem, raised in the South Bronx,
went to public school, got out of public college, went into the Army,
and then I just stuck with it."
—Colin Powell

"Some people like chaos and others structure.
I like the latter."
—Christy Turlington

"I'm not going to deny it. I'm a neat person, there's no question."
—Courteney Cox

"I didn't care about being the 'star.' I just wanted to make a living
and have a consistent career."
—Angie Dickinson

"Winning the prize wasn't half as exciting
as doing the work itself."
—Maria Goeppert-Mayer, recipient of the 1963 Nobel Prize in Physics

"People without information cannot act responsibly."
—Ken Blanchard

"I prefer tongue-tied knowledge to ignorant loquacity."
—Cicero

"I have a resistance to change in things that I feel
comfortable with and that I'm used to."
—Dennis Quaid

"Work hard and play by the rules."
—Al Gore

"Change is never easy."
–Sally Field

"People are always telling me that change is good. But all that means is that something you didn't want to happen has happened."
—Meg Ryan

"I could prove God statistically. Take the human body alone— the chances that all the functions of an individual would just happen is a statistical monstrosity."
—George Gallup

"It's the quality of the ordinary, the straight, the square, that accounts for the great stability and success of our nation. It's a quality to be proud of. But it's a quality that many people seem to have neglected."
—President Gerald R. Ford

Communication Style

Stabilizers tend to communicate in a measured, even tone. Even when irritated or angered, Stabilizers try to be controlled in their responses. They usually do not reveal a great deal of themselves, and the more pressure they experience, the more they hold back. They tend to communicate with words like "I think" or "I believe," rather than "I feel."

Stabilizers typically react to new ideas with skepticism. They have a propensity to envision the worst-case scenario, and will voice their

concerns about perceived problems. They plan for the future by analyzing the present, so if you want to influence them you must come
armed with information. Stabilizers base their beliefs, actions, and
ideas on what they can prove to be true.

When Communicating with Stabilizers

❑ You'll need to have the facts, and lots of them. You cannot motivate
Stabilizers by sheer enthusiasm alone.

❑ Stabilizers have to believe a thing is doable, workable, and logical
in order to get on board with a new vision. You must give them
enough factual evidence to enlist their support.

❑ When you present data, do so systematically. Stabilizers like to have
information communicated to them in an orderly, organized way.

❑ When explaining concepts, use facts and figures rather than word
pictures or stories.

Cognitive Process

Stabilizers are analytical and methodical. They tend to be better with
numbers than with words. Stabilizers think in a rational, linear way.
They value their ability to think clearly and dislike being challenged
about their conclusions.

Stabilizers are systematic thinkers. They want to know all the details
before making a decision, and they look for patterns. Their thought
processes tend to be sequential and associative. They see links that others miss. They perceive what is missing or out of order. Inconsistencies
jump out at them.

My husband, Peter, is a Stabilizer. Our staff is in awe of his analytical
abilities. Recently, our accountant passed a spreadsheet to Peter, and as
it was coming across the desk *upside down,* Peter said, "The third num-

ber in the fourth column is wrong." The accountant laughed, thinking that Peter was joking, but he wasn't. The number was incorrect.

Stabilizers are able to decipher complex data and understand confusing information. They are intellectually inquisitive. It's not enough for them to know that something works; they also have to know *how* it works. They like to take things apart and figure out what makes them tick.

Likely Strengths

- ❏ Thoroughness and attention to detail
- ❏ Defining and refining ideas
- ❏ Ability to carry tasks through to completion
- ❏ Analyzing problems and determining what needs to be done
- ❏ The ability to mentally organize their thoughts
- ❏ Reliable and consistent
- ❏ Skilled at sorting out priorities

Possible Pitfalls

When focused on a project, Stabilizers can come across as too intense or aloof. Easily frustrated when people ignore the rules, Stabilizers can be seen as strict, starched, and inflexible. In order to effectively connect with others, Stabilizers may need to refine their communication skills.

Stabilizers seek perfection and can be somewhat obsessive in their quest for the ideal. They also run the risk of not simply seeking perfection but actually becoming perfectionists. Sometimes pedantic and nitpicky, their deliberations may persist to the point of exhausting others. When others are ready to act, Stabilizers may put on the brakes and draw attention to yet another unforeseen obstacle.

Stabilizers usually evaluate risks accurately. However, they tend to be overly cautious about opportunities. If permitted to lead a team or process, Stabilizers tend to choose low-risk initiatives while squelching ideas that are more risky but also have larger payoffs.

Stabilizers at Work

Meticulous in their work, Stabilizers are intent on analyzing situations and staying on track. They prioritize their various tasks and activities, and are prompt and prepared for meetings. Stabilizers like a well-organized approach to work goals. They want the information needed to reach team goals, preferably at the beginning of the process. Stabilizers expect that the necessary resources needed to do the job will be readily available to them and are frustrated or resentful when they are not.

Stabilizers are uncomfortable submitting work that isn't as good as it could be. As a result, it may take them longer than other people to do their work, because they are so scrupulous and thorough. Stabilizers are conscious of their own work ethic and high performance standards. They realize that they work hard and find it insufferable when their coworkers don't do the same. They like neatness and efficiency in the work product of others. Haphazard, halfhearted work is particularly exasperating to them, especially when they have to go back and correct the errors that others overlooked. Stabilizers hate lazy, sloppy thinking. They want others to be as focused and mentally disciplined as they are.

Feeling driven by the pressures of the day, Stabilizers get upset when their work piles up. In order to do their best work, they need sufficient time alone to think, strategize, and prepare. Stabilizers like to review the previous history of a project and adequately plan for future actions.

They need time at the end of the day to plan the next day's priorities. Inefficiency drives them mad. Stabilizers can't function in disorder and chaos. An uncluttered environment enables them to work with a clear head. When everything is in its place, they are content.

Uncomfortable with rapid change, Stabilizers prefer that the structure and objectives of the organization remain relatively unchanged. As long as they do it well, Stabilizers expect any job they hold or any responsibility they have to be theirs for as long as they want it. Stabilizers desire job security and a work environment that remains fairly constant.

Stabilizers don't require a lot of supervision. Give them freedom, peace and quiet, and the chance to do their thing. They will expect detailed direction about what to do, how to do it, when it needs to be done, and what resources will be available to them. After receiving that information, Stabilizers desire the autonomy to get the job done. As long as they know the organization's goals, they are focused in their determination to achieve them.

When Working with Stabilizers

- ❑ Give them detailed instructions and clear objectives.
- ❑ Supply them with ongoing support.
- ❑ Avoid pressuring them with unreasonable deadlines.
- ❑ Do not micromanage them.
- ❑ Tell the Stabilizer how much he is needed and how the job couldn't be done properly without him.
- ❑ Allow Stabilizers time to work at their own pace.
- ❑ Recognize and reward their diligence.
- ❑ Submit new ideas cautiously.
- ❑ Stabilizers become stressed by sudden or unexpected change. Don't change gears too quickly with Stabilizers. They need time to process a new idea or course of action.

Stabilizers at Play

Stabilizers prefer to postpone play and get their work done first. Anything that is left undone weighs heavily on them and they have a hard time relaxing until the task is completed. They often impose restrictions on themselves, such as having to finish a project before they go home or go out to enjoy themselves.

Stabilizers enjoy downtime with family and friends, but their responsible nature often causes them to defer social events until their work is complete. When they do play, Stabilizers enjoy structuring their time to make the most out of it. They are famous for planning every moment of a vacation or outing in exacting detail.

Stabilizers in Relationships

Stabilizers can be hard to get to know. They are not usually open or outgoing until they get acquainted with someone. People sometimes misread their restrained nature as unsympathetic or distant. However, once a Stabilizer knows and trusts someone, he or she is intensely loyal to the other person.

When Dealing with Stabilizers

1. Stabilizers expect others to show respect for authority and play by the rules.
2. Compliments and public displays of affection can embarrass them.
3. They do not like being rushed in decision making, especially for important choices that have long-term consequences. Stabilizers like to take things one step at a time.

4. Stabilizers need to be financially secure, with their bills paid on time. If you are married to a Stabilizer, you must honor their need for financial order.

5. They are prone to give practical gifts rather than romantic ones, but this doesn't mean they aren't romantic. They just express their love in practical ways.

6. Stabilizers practice what they preach—they don't expect from others what they are unwilling or unable to do themselves.

7. Appreciate them for all their wonderful traits—don't focus on the one or two things that bother you. Remember that the whole world would be a chaotic mess without Stabilizers.

Resolving Conflict

Stabilizers are responsible citizens. Right and wrong are very important to them. If you are wrong, you do well to admit it up front. Otherwise, you will reach an impasse with Stabilizers because they will fight to the death in defense of the truth as they see it. An impassioned argument will not move a Stabilizer, but a logical one will. Before you confront them, think through your line of reasoning.

How Stabilizers Influence Others

It's hard to argue with the facts, and Stabilizers are data-driven, fact-finding machines. They influence others by making a compelling, rational case. Their reasoned and well-researched approach will often effectively sway their peers.

Value to Organization

Stabilizers excel at organization. They ensure that concepts are thought through and determine how ideas can be improved. They work hard to eliminate waste and redundancy. Stabilizers don't want time or resources to be squandered. They hate fraud, cheating, stealing, and lack of integrity. Desiring excellence and economy, Stabilizers are good at both quality control and cost control.

De-Motivators

Stabilizers become de-motivated when they are forced to work with incompetent people and coworkers who don't work as hard or who won't carry their fair share of responsibility. For a time, Stabilizers may take on all the work themselves, but they will quickly become bitter and lose motivation. Ultimately, it will adversely affect their ability to do their work. When people try to take the easy way out, Stabilizers get irritated. Their motto is: "Do it right or give it to someone who can."

Stabilizers lose enthusiasm when they have to work with inefficient systems. It frustrates them when things don't make sense. They want all the i's dotted, all the t's crossed, and all the ducks lined up. They can grow exasperated when inefficiencies are not addressed despite their objections. Likewise, when others ignore their well-thought-out plans, Stabilizers can become demoralized.

Top Ten Motivators

1. Rhythm, routine, consistency, and predictability
2. Time to think and process data

3. Verbal appreciation for their hard work
4. Clearly defined objectives
5. Understanding the big picture, the "why" behind what they do
6. Order and organization
7. Competent coworkers
8. Clear, reasonable deadlines
9. Being heard and understood
10. The necessary tools to get the job done

Advice for Stabilizers

Few things happen in your life until you create the space for it. Carve out time to have fun and relax. Schedule short breaks in your day. Push away from the tyranny of the urgent. Don't allow yourself to get stuck in the rut of routine. Become comfortable with being uncomfortable. Remember that Stability does not mean immobility.

Practice editing your thoughts when communicating with Producers and Variables. Work on becoming a motivator of others. People need affirmation, not just instruction. At work and at home, make it a habit to point out what has been done correctly, not merely what needs to be fixed.

FREE BONUS #7
The Success Toolkit featuring 20 Organizational Forms
and Tools to Help You Manage Your Life and
Prioritize Your Tasks. ($69 value)

A dream without a plan is a *wish*—but a dream with a plan is an unstoppable combination. These forms, checklists, questions, and strategic inventories will help you *find* the magnetic north for your personal and professional life and *follow* it on a daily basis.

How to Gain the Bounce-Back Confidence of Variables

"George Foreman: A miracle. A mystery to myself. Who am I?
The mirror says back, 'The George you was always meant to be.'"
—GEORGE FOREMAN

I love George Foreman. I'm not the world's biggest boxing enthusiast, but I am a genuine fan of the man. He is smart, funny, gregarious, hardworking, and principled—a truly good man.

George is also a uniquely talented athlete. At the age of nineteen, he startled the world by winning the gold medal in boxing at the 1968 Olympics in Mexico City. Soon after, he became the most feared challenger in pro boxing, going undefeated through forty fights—winning more than half of them in the first two rounds. Then, in 1973, as the underdog against world champion Joe Frazier, Foreman shocked everyone by capturing the world heavyweight title.

George went on to become an ordained minister and pastor. Then, at the age of forty-five, he defied the odds and silenced the critics when he made history by reclaiming his title as heavyweight champion of the world and became the oldest boxer ever to win the title.

From world heavyweight champion to lean, mean grilling machine entrepreneur, George Foreman has proven that he is a winner both in and out of the ring. He is a sports hero, a spiritual leader, a family man, father of ten, businessman, and entertainment icon.

I love this photo of George and me. It always makes me smile. There is no mistaking that both of us are Variables. In fact, in the fifteen years I've known George, I don't have a single "normal" photo of the two of us together. George is always mugging or grimacing for the camera. I finally gave up on capturing a conventional shot. Now I just clown around with him.

George can be a ham, a common trait among Variables. Variables love being the center of attention. Whether he is speaking as a preacher or a prime-time pitchman, George has an obvious flair for communication. He is always a crowd favorite at our GET MOTIVATED Business Seminars.

Most professional public speakers hone their message down to a polished thirty- or sixty-minute presentation and repeat it for audiences everywhere they go. George changes his presentation every time he speaks—and believe me, every message is a knockout.

Right before George and I took this picture, he signed the glove he was wearing with the words "If you could just get your hand in this glove, you can do as I did." When I introduced him in Houston, Texas, to 18,000 enthusiastic fans, he held up the glove and explained the inscription: "I want you to see something about this. This is just not just any glove. This today is the glove of all gloves—because I just put my left hand into it."

The audience laughed. George continued, "If you can get your hand in this glove, you can do as I did. Today, tomorrow, if you're depressed or have lost a job, you just slip this glove on, and you will feel the same power and the same thrill and the same sense of courage that I feel right now! You can jump up and conquer the world!"

As the audience applauded, George grinned. "Did I sell ya?"

The crowd yelled back, "YES!"

"Good! You see, if you learn how to sell, you'll never starve."

Later in the day, I saw the champ backstage. I said, "George, you did a great job! And you know what? You sold me too! If I could just get my hand in that glove . . ." George laughed, reached into his bag, and produced the glove of all gloves. "Tamara, it's yours," he said. "I was gonna give it to you this morning, but I had to sell you on it first!"

Temperament

Variables are persuasive and convincing. As a result, they tend to be influential. They have a passion for personal growth and self-expression. Their playful nature brings out the fun in others. Variables have a way of making ordinary things seem exciting. They tend to be confident and outgoing and are energized by exploration.

Variables love change and live for adventure. They are fun-loving freethinkers who seek out new experiences and don't shy away from risk. They tend to be entrepreneurial and find change stimulating rather than taxing.

What Variables tend to dislike are details, routines, and strict organization (the very things that stimulate Stabilizers). Variables feel confined by excessive structure and bureaucracy. They prefer things to be kept on a casual basis, without too much formality. Variables will go to great lengths to ensure that they have flexibility and options. They are spontaneous and impulsive. They can change their minds or direction on a dime. Variables tend to jump into things and think about the consequences while free-falling.

Confident in their ability to master new skills, Variables are lifelong learners. They view life as a journey of learning and discovery. Variables think that everything revolves around personal growth. There never seems to be enough time to pursue all the activities and educational experiences available to them. I'm a Variable myself, and I can tell you that we Variables often have trouble choosing a course of action. There are so many exciting and interesting possibilities that capture our attention.

The Thrill-Seeking Variable

As a Variable, I have an unquenchable thirst for adventure. I've had the opportunity to travel to more than seventy countries. I've ridden a camel and explored the pyramids in Cairo, Egypt. I've climbed to the top of Machu Picchu, the "Lost City of the Incas" in Peru. Shrouded by clouds, these spectacular ruins are located at an altitude of almost 8,000 feet, at the top of a mountain peak that towers above the gorgeous Urubamba Valley.

In Mexico, I fed sharks by hand after being lowered in a Plexiglas cube beneath the ocean's surface. One of the greatest highs I've ever had was swimming with dolphins in the Grand Caymans. The experience was so exciting, I couldn't sleep that night. I've been charged by a rhino—twice: once while riding on an elephant when I was on safari in Nepal, and again last summer in South Africa. I've watched monkeys swing limb to limb, flying and tumbling through the treetops in the jungles of India. I've trekked through Europe and explored the biblical sites of the Holy Land.

But there was one adventure that I will never forget—much as I wish I could. Just thinking about it makes my heart palpitate and my hands sweat, a decade later. I was in Zimbabwe, Africa, at the end of a ten-country speaking tour. To celebrate, I wanted to do something adventurous. I had planned to go whitewater rafting on the Zambezi River. It's Class V and is considered some of the best whitewater in the world. However, the evening I arrived in Zimbabwe I discovered that the Zambezi was contaminated with bilharzia, a tropical disease caused by parasitic worms. That was a little too adventurous for me, although in retrospect I probably would have been safer going on the raft trip.

The next morning, I found myself atop a narrow strip of metal called Victoria Falls Bridge. I was engulfed in the mist of the world's largest waterfall as it raged all around me. The noise of Victoria Falls was a deafening thunder as water cascaded over the cliffs, crashing down more than 300 feet to the Zambezi River below. Mist exploded over 1,000 feet into the air as the river roared through the gorge.

"Tamara, are you ready?"

"Huh? For what?"

"Are you ready to jump?"

A few African teenagers were running an operation described as "The World's Longest Bungee Jump." For some reason that I cannot explain to this day, I allowed them to equip me with a bungee harness. Actually, that sounds far more impressive than it really was. The so-called bungee harness was essentially a couple of raggedy towels bound around my ankles, covered with a thin strip of Velcro, and attached to a fraying elastic cord. I surveyed the washcloth and rubber band wrapped around my feet.

"Is that it?" I said. "You must be kidding! Is this thing safe?"

The boys started laughing. Not a good sign.

"No, seriously, has anybody ever died doing this?"

"You're going to be fine," one of the teenagers said as he helped me hobble out onto a metal plank attached to the bridge. The platform had no rails. It was a diving board overhanging eternity. The plank was shaking and vibrating in the wind; I feared it would collapse beneath my weight.

I thought, *If I die, they probably won't even call the police. They'll just cut bait and run.*

I gazed at the swirling abyss below.

"Don't look down!" the boy commanded.

"This is crazy! Dear God, birds are flying *below* us!"

The young man ignored me. He said, "When I count to three, you jump."

"No way! I can't do this!"

"ONE! TWO! THREEEEEE!"

Out of the blue an empowering thought occurs to me: I am a stuntwoman in an action movie. The cameras are rolling—and I'm going to do this in one clean take!

I spread my arms, take a deep breath, lean forward . . . and execute a flaw-less, gold-medal-winning, perfect swan dive off the platform. I hear the people on the bridge clapping and cheering.

"You're a stupid stuntwoman!" The shrill wind shrieks in my ears, mock-ing me, as I plunge earthward toward the churning river. The water races toward me; the cliffs on both sides are just a blur. I am plummeting to my inescapable, bone-shattering demise.

Suddenly, everything stops. Not a sound. Not a breath. I am suspended in space and time. The cord recoils, yanking me upward about 100 feet. I am flying skyward. Flying and falling, up and down, over the falls. Then I'm left dangling like a worm on a fishing line, gaping at the wondrous upside-down world.

One of the boys lowers himself on a rope from the bridge, hooks on to my harness, and hoists me back up.

"How was it?" he asked.

I was speechless and shaking. It was FANTASTIC—and I will never, ever do anything like that again.

When I got back to terra firma, the guys operating the bungee jump gathered around to high-five and congratulate me. They said it was the one of the best dives they'd ever seen. My bungee-jumping experience serves to illustrate one of the hallmark traits of the Variable: insane confidence. If we can't do something, we just act like we can—and do it anyway!

VARIABLES IN THEIR OWN WORDS

"My theory is that if you look confident you can pull off anything—even if you have no clue what you're doing."
—Jessica Alba

"Not only do I knock 'em out, I pick the round."
—Muhammad Ali

"I just have more fun when I get to try new things."
—Bruce Willis

"I feel very adventurous. There are so many doors to be opened, and I'm not afraid to look behind them."
—Elizabeth Taylor

"I've found that every time I've made a radical change, it's helped me feel buoyant as an artist."
—David Bowie

"I've done all this stuff because it's fun. It's never been about fame."
—Elle Macpherson

"Just play. Have fun. Enjoy the game."
—Michael Jordan

"You just have to be confident, and you might be wrong,
but sell it anyway."
—Lisa Kudrow

"Challenge yourself. You'll like the change."
—Jenny Craig

"I knew early on that the news business was right for me.
I enjoyed it. It was fun. If I thought it was work,
I might not have done it."
—Sam Donaldson

"This is a fantastic time to be entering the business world,
because business is going to change more in the next ten years
than it has in the last fifty."
—Bill Gates

"I'm a person who's learning a lot.
Always and forever learning."
—Alicia Keys

Communication Style

Variables usually communicate in an expressive, upbeat way. They are talkative and animated. Variables often have an engaging, open candidness that is irresistibly magnetic. They have an ability to establish rapport quickly. They can be captivating and flirtatious in a way that can instantly connect them with others. Their humor, energy, and gusto for life tend to win people over. Quick-witted and entertaining, they often use humor to break the ice.

Their dynamic and vibrant style sets them apart from other people. They are natural performers with a flair for the dramatic. Variables are able to convincingly convey their thoughts and feelings. They can be great storytellers, regaling others with anecdotes and adding embellishments that grow with each retelling.

Variables are happy to share their thoughts and feelings—anywhere, anytime—whether invited or not. Every subject is fair game. They have difficulty masking what they think or feel. It all comes spilling out. Opinionated and passionate, Variables find themselves at home in the middle of any conversation. They are candid and expressive, telling it like it is. They do not intend to be rude and are often surprised when others are occasionally upset by their outspokenness.

When Communicating with Variables
- ❏ Be positive and enthusiastic.
- ❏ Maintain eye contact and be a good listener.
- ❏ Show interest in their opinions.
- ❏ Express your appreciation of their achievements.
- ❏ When explaining concepts, use visuals, word pictures, or demonstrations. Variables are hands-on learners.
- ❏ Use stories and illustrations rather than facts and figures to convince them of your point of view.

Cognitive Process

Variables are imaginative, original thinkers and are good at finding creative solutions. They delight in creativity and the process of discovery. Variables have an intuitive intelligence. They tend to make decisions based on emotions and "gut feelings," rather than facts alone. They are apt to be better with words than numbers. Variables love change—

including the inclination to change their minds quickly. They are naturally curious and love learning new things.

Variables become detached when forced to analyze at length. They experience analysis fatigue. Variables are farsighted futurists who have more ideas than time to execute them. Their generation of ideas can seem like water shooting out of a fire hose, forceful and plentiful. Others sometimes see them as disorganized and scattered. They have a limitless range of interests and are stimulated by whatever is new and innovative.

Likely Strengths

❏ The ability to persuade or influence others
❏ Creative problem solving
❏ The ability to negotiate
❏ Articulating a vision that inspires team buy-in
❏ Mobilizing others to action

Possible Pitfalls

Variables tend to underanalyze risk. They are inclined to be impulsive and make snap decisions. Variables can be too eager to instigate change in a cautious environment. They are thrill seekers and need to balance their impulsiveness with someone who will act as a stabilizer or voice of reason for them.

Variables can be loud, self-centered, and overly talkative, especially about their favorite subject: themselves. They may lack focus and be undisciplined. Variables tend to have a short attention span and can have difficulty staying focused on one task for a long time. They wrestle with organized structure and achieving a balanced life.

Variables tend to undertake the quick, easy, and enjoyable tasks first while delaying or ignoring unpleasant tasks. It often takes pressure from an approaching deadline to get them started doing the chores they dislike. Variables may also have difficulty with follow-through. They can be easily distracted. Variables tend to begin projects with a burst of enthusiasm and often bring them to the brink of completion before abandoning them out of boredom.

Variables are inclined to shun supervision and question authority. They rebel against too much control and may sulk when constrained. They resist standard operating procedures and look for ways to do things differently. Where a rule exists, they are bound to break it.

Variables at Work

Variables enjoy having a lot of balls in the air. Their ability to juggle multiple tasks and projects is commendable; however, they may lack attention to detail and need help managing priorities. Variables excel in creative environments that allow them to innovate. Their gift of gab and power of persuasion make them naturals in sales and marketing. They are also energetic leaders who enjoy taking on new assignments.

When Working with Variables
❏ Allow them the freedom to find creative solutions.
❏ Invite them to participate in brainstorming sessions.
❏ Challenge Variables with a goal—then let them figure out how to accomplish it.
❏ Provide accountability and deadlines.
❏ Offer them opportunities for personal and professional growth.
❏ Give them public recognition for their accomplishments.

❏ Variables get bored easily, so when they finish a project have another one ready.

❏ Invite them to talk about their ideas.

Variables at Play

Variables are all about play. They have an insatiable hunger for new experiences. They are inclined to try high-risk sports. They are interested in sampling everything—new foods, exotic destinations, and unique experiences. Variables are generally ahead of the curve on the latest trends and ideas.

Variables in Relationships

Because of their short attention spans, Variables can be perceived as commitment-phobic. This is generally not true. Variables enjoy relationships, but their core need is for fun, new experiences, and an unending supply of excitement. They hate being in a rut, and when the excitement of a new relationship wears off, their enthusiasm wanes. Feed their need for fun and Variables light up.

Resolving Conflict with Variables

It is generally not difficult to resolve conflicts with Variables, because they are naturally inclined to resolution. Typically, Variables are conciliatory and eager to restore fractured relationships. If you don't know how to solve a conflict, ask a Variable—he or she will come up with a dozen ideas without breaking a sweat.

How Variables Influence Others

Variables have a way of making others feel like they are a part of the in-crowd. Strangers warm to them instantly. People may feel mysteriously connected to them, as though they have known them for a long time, even if they have just met. Variables tend to be extremely effective communicators and are able to drum up the passion of a group and direct it toward a goal or vision. Their enthusiasm, optimism, and clarity of expression energize others to rally to the causes they promote.

Value to Organization

Variables have an enviable ability to articulate a vision and create a climate of excitement to achieve organizational goals. They love to get others excited about their passions. Their zeal and certainty ensure buy-in from the rest of the group.

Powerful morale boosters, Variables can lift the spirits of the entire team. They provide strong support and encouragement to others and serve as positive, can-do cheerleaders. Variables have a gift for sales and persuasion. They are so believable and convincing that they inspire the confidence of others. Their ability to slip into character on either side of an issue also makes them natural negotiators.

Variables look for fresh, innovative concepts that go beyond the obvious. If there is a better way of doing something, Variables will find it. They don't feel obligated to follow institutional tradition. Variables envision solutions that may shake up the status quo. They seek new ways of seeing and doing things outside the constraints of convention.

De-Motivators

When a project ceases to be fun, Variables lose enthusiasm for the task or activity. Unlike Stabilizers, who responsibly finish an assignment no matter how tedious it may be, Variables will stop mid-project without a second thought.

Variables also despise repetitive tasks. Rules and regulations irritate them. The freedom to choose their own course is essential to their sense of well-being. Variables believe that going by the book isn't always the best course of action. They think of rules as suggestions. They don't think of themselves as breaking the rules, but improving them.

Variables enjoy an element of surprise and dislike planning ahead for every contingency. Too much structure, detail, and minutiae can turn them off.

Top Ten Motivators

1. Adventure and change
2. Relaxed schedule and flexible deadlines
3. Learning new skills
4. Being the center of attention
5. The chance to explore new ideas
6. Options
7. Varied job responsibilities
8. The power to adapt or alter tasks, schedules, procedures, etc.
9. A creative work environment
10. Opportunities for personal growth

Advice for Variables

Set a goal to tackle at least one unpleasant task every day. Practice the art of sustained focus. Finish the task and don't quit until it is done. Resist the impulse to continually switch projects. Concentrate on follow-through.

Think about how you can eliminate distractions and interruptions in order to stay focused. For example, you may want to rearrange your office furniture so you don't face the door or see the traffic flow. Organize your environment for better efficiency.

Be careful not to monopolize conversations. Give others the opportunity to share their opinions. Ask questions about them and their interests. Show respect for others by being punctual. Think about how your spontaneity could adversely affect those who need structure and like to adhere to schedules. Being on time and keeping your commitments communicates to others that you respect them.

FREE BONUS #8
Executive Book Summaries of Ten Business Bestsellers
to Help You Advance in Your Career. ($85 value)

Leaders are learners . . . and learners are earners! Your next book bonus gives you the most important points and the most useful information from ten bestselling career strategy books:

- *Career Intensity* by David Lorenzo
- *Business Class* by Jacqueline Whitmore
- *The 7 Habits of Highly Successful People* by Stephen R. Covey
- *The 8th Habit* by Stephen R. Covey
- *Winning* by Jack Welch
- *What Color Is Your Parachute?* by Richard Bolles
- *Working with Emotional Intelligence* by Daniel Goleman
- *Career Warfare* by David D'Alessandro
- *From Success to Significance* by Lloyd Reeb
- *The Brand Called You* by Peter Montoya and Tim Vandehey

What Internals Know About the Meaning of Life

"The miracle is not that we do this work,
but that we are happy to do it."
—MOTHER TERESA

I n Calcutta, India, fourteen million people live in deplorable poverty. Rats outnumber people eight to one. Children scavenge for food in the garbage. An open sewer runs through the streets and the stench is unbearable. In the midst of this heartbreaking chaos, Mother Teresa created calm. She administered help to the suffering and comfort to the dying. The work was not a burden to her; she did it joyfully. In truth, Mother Teresa was the most contented person I have ever known.

"Tamara," she once told me, "spread love everywhere you go. Let no one come to you without leaving happier. A short, kind word is easy to speak, but its echo is endless. Money is not enough. Do not be satisfied with just giving money. What people really need is to be loved. Spread your love everywhere you go."

Mother Teresa was a saint long before the Catholic Church recognized her as one.

I had the wonderful privilege of working with Mother Teresa and assisting her ministry at the Missionaries of Charity Nirmal Hriday Home for the Dying in India. It is an experience that I am profoundly grateful for and one that marked my life in a very deep way.

Mother Teresa was the greatest example of an Internal that I have ever known. People with an Internal Award system are "mission minded." They are idealists who seek to make a positive contribution. Fueled by a longing to make the world a better place, Internals yearn to be involved with significant projects. Mother Teresa worked with the sick and the dying and the poorest of the poor because she was compelled to help. She didn't do it for money—she did it for spiritual reasons. She was motivated by compassion. Yet, in a grand providential paradox, her vow of poverty made her rich. Service to the suffering enriched her soul.

Like Mother Teresa, Internals tend to be altruistic individuals. The fulfillment and personal satisfaction they find in making a difference eclipse personal gain. This is not to say that money is *unimportant* to them, it's just not *the most important* thing. Everybody wants to be paid a fair wage for their work, but Internals are motivated by outcome rather than income. They're less concerned about making a buck than they are about making a difference.

Temperament

Internals are defined by the strong values that guide their lives. Personal integrity is paramount for Internals. Purpose and fulfillment are more significant to them than fame and fortune. They know what they believe and they live those beliefs. Their firm sense of purpose, and their values, compels them to do work that they find meaningful and important. They want to feel that they are part of something bigger than themselves.

Personal contribution is essential to their happiness. Internals are generous with material possessions and willing to share whatever they have. An unselfish readiness to volunteer when needed is characteristic of them. Internals like the feeling of being involved. They are sensitive to the feelings and concerns of others and are motivated by a desire to make things better.

Often active in politics, Internals are aware of and attentive to the socioeconomic issues of the day. Visionary, farsighted, and idealistic, they believe it is their responsibility to right injustice. They are genuinely concerned about the well-being of others and are willing to fight for the downtrodden.

Internals have clearly defined beliefs about what is right and wrong. They are usually fair and unbiased. They have the courage of their convictions and the guts to stand up for what they believe in, despite opposition. They enjoy helping to improve the quality of people's lives and assisting people who can't help themselves.

Internals are willing to rise above self-interest. They will set aside their own needs if necessary to achieve the greater good. They want to use their skills and abilities to initiate transformation, lend a hand, and make things better. Internals often aspire to have their work outlive them, and they are committed to accomplishing something that endures.

The Mission-Minded Internal

Our seminar attendees usually do a double take when they see the pierced and tattooed ruffians in business suits who staff our events. Dreadlocks, goatees, and eyebrow piercings aren't typical trappings of the corporate world. What you probably don't know is that those well-dressed hippies are actually humanitarians in disguise. They are part of a relief organization that provides food, clothing, and drug counseling to the Rainbow People. And who are the Rainbow People? you might ask. They seldom attract national media coverage and most folks have never heard of them, but the Rainbow Family represent a huge counterculture of social dropouts who live off the land.

A loose-knit troupe of more than 60,000 vagabonds, beatniks, teenage runaways, Deadheads, New Agers, radical environmentalists, Pagans, earth-worshippers, peace activists, and drug addicts, the Rainbow People wander the country and congregate in the woods. Most live in tents or battered vehicles as they migrate from one Rainbow gathering to the next.

Rainbow Family participants say that their group is "the largest non-organization of non-members in the world," and playfully call themselves a "disorganization." There are no official leaders or structure, no Web site, no official spokespersons, and no formalized membership. As far as the general public is concerned, these are people who have dropped off the face of the earth—and that's why they've probably never been a blip on your radar until now.

Living much like the hippies and flower children of the 1960s, today's transients sustain themselves with little or no money. Disillusioned and disenfranchised from society, they flock to the forests to share campfires, tribal drumming, sex, drugs, and what little food they can scrounge together.

My friend Joshua Hanson, a former Rainbow kid himself, says, "They are all really searching and seeking. Most of them are really spiritual people. And they are surviving on the waste of America, eating out of dumpsters. They have backpacks and hitchhike and get around on next to nothing."

Joshua is the leader of the Rainbow relief workers who help staff our seminar events. The money they earn at the GET MOTIVATED Seminars is channeled back into their volunteer work. Josh, his wife, Shallyn, their two young sons, and their team travel the United States in brightly painted buses and RVs. They run a program that provides food from their houses-on-wheels, helping to feed thousands of Rainbow People each year.

Josh says, "I know what it's like to be without hope and without purpose. I did all these peace walks and shamanic journeys. I lived with the Krishnas and traveled around the world, looking for meaning. I did all kinds of drugs. I'd get drunk first, then try about anything anyone put in front of me."

I asked Josh how he went from being one of the Rainbow kids to getting clean and being in a position to help them. "Well, we ran into some Christians who were out feeding the homeless," Josh said. "We stopped to get something to eat and talk to them, and this lady named Hazel told us about how she was saved. We all had head lice, and Hazel took us back to her home and debugged us. She washed all our clothes and helped us get clean. She really loved on us."

That was 1998, and it marked the beginning of Josh's turnaround. In 2001, he founded the nonprofit Jesus Loves You Ministries to help the teenagers and young adults who make up 80 percent of the Rainbow Family. He began with one little Toyota van and has since built a mobile community with thirty to forty people traveling the country in seven buses and RVs. "We have a free kitchen and we set up a camp where we give away free food, clothing, and supplies. A lot of the Rainbows are HIV-positive because of the promiscuity, drugs, and needle use. We spend months of the year in the woods to help these kids and be their friends."

I wanted you to hear Joshua Hanson's story not only to illustrate the Internal award system at work, but also because Josh's outreach to the Rainbow People is one of more than thirty not-for-profit relief organizations and children's charities that the sales of this book are assisting. One hundred percent of the author proceeds of this book are being donated to charity. On behalf of all the people you are helping and the great causes supported by your purchase of *Get Motivated!*, allow me to say "Thank you!" For a listing of the nonprofit charities we have partnered with, please see Appendix C or visit www.GetMotivatedBook.com.

An All-Star Motivator

I want to tell you about another Internal who has had a major impact on my life: Pat Williams. You may recognize him as the senior vice president of the NBA's Orlando Magic. Twenty-three of his teams have gone to the NBA playoffs and five have made the Finals. Pat Williams has been named one of the fifty most influential people in NBA history. But his basketball career has not been easy. "The expectations and demands are so high. Man, it's like we need a miracle every night," Pat says. "Every team has to go 82–0 or we're not happy. It's like a nervous breakdown with a paycheck!"

Being a basketball executive is a big part of his life, but it's not the only thing Pat does. Williams is also the author of forty-five books, and he hosts three weekly radio shows. In the past twelve years he has completed forty-two marathons, including the Boston Marathon, which he has run eleven times. Williams is a former U.S. Army soldier and Minor League catcher, a serious weightlifter, a Civil War buff, and has climbed Mount Rainier. As you may suspect by now, Pat is a Producer and a Variable, but he is also an Internal.

As admirable as his accomplishments are, Pat's greatest achievement has been in the realm of parenting. Did you know that Pat Williams and his wife, Ruth, are the parents of nineteen children? Fourteen of their kids were adopted from foreign countries. One year, he and his wife had sixteen teenagers at the same time. "That was the year I bought into the Mark Twain philosophy of raising teenagers," Pat says with a laugh. "Twain said, 'When your child reaches thirteen, you put them in a barrel. Cut a hole in the barrel to feed them. And then, at sixteen . . . seal up the hole!'"

When I asked Pat why he and his wife adopted so many children, he said, "There was no program—no plan. As we learned about these kids, we just answered, 'Yes.'"

Reflecting on the challenges of parenthood, Pat said, "It's very demanding—very hard. And, of course, there's the challenge of time, but we made the time. We always tried to be together at breakfast. I did everything I could to be there for all their sporting events. That's *twenty-one years* of Little League baseball. I've seen more youth sporting events than any dad in history! To do that, it means you've got to give up some stuff—no golf, no fishing trips. They needed me to be there."

That last statement encapsulates the driving motivation of all Internals: "They needed me to be there."

INTERNALS IN THEIR OWN WORDS

"Don't ever take a job for the money or a title. . . .
I would go for a cause anytime versus a job."
—Colleen Barrett, President and COO, Southwest Airlines

"Watching women achieve their dreams is
the thing that keeps me inspired."
—Mary Kay Ash

"Try not to become a person of success, but rather
a person of value."
—Albert Einstein

"Anywhere I see suffering, that is where I want to be,
doing what I can."
—Princess Diana

"We make a living by what we get, but we make a life
by what we give."
—Winston Churchill

"There is more to life than increasing its speed."
—Mahatma Gandhi

"I don't think the money people in Hollywood have ever thought I
was normal, but I am dedicated to my work and that's what counts.
I've been reckless, but I'm not a rebel without a cause."
—Angelina Jolie

"Everybody can be great . . . because anybody can serve.
You don't have to have a college degree to serve. You don't have to
make your subject and verb agree to serve. You only need
a heart full of grace. A soul generated by love."
—Martin Luther King, Jr.

"The best index to a person's character is how he treats people
who can't do him any good, and how he treats
people who can't fight back."
—Abigail Van Buren

"You have to stand for what you believe in, and
sometimes you have to stand alone."
—Queen Latifah

Communication Style

Internals are empathetic and their communication style reflects that. They are most animated about the issues they have a passion for. Internals are able to rouse people to contribute to the causes they care about and inspire others to take meaningful action.

When Communicating with Internals
- ❑ Express interest in their interests.
- ❑ Use words like "feel," "believe," and "value" to communicate your views.
- ❑ Explain the purpose of tasks and show why it matters.
- ❑ Look for areas of agreement; when you find those common elements, tell them, "I feel the same way."
- ❑ Allow them the freedom to voice their opinions without dissent.
- ❑ Affirm their viewpoint before stating your own.

Cognitive Process

Internals want to know the "why" before they figure out the "how." They like to see the big picture first and then understand how all the pieces fit together. Internals trust their own judgment. Believing that principles are the core strength of a society, Internals behave in a way that is consistent with their personal values.

Even if the news is bad, Internals think honesty is the best policy. They are honest with themselves and others and are determined to stick to their principles even when it's easier not to. They accept responsibility for their actions and expect others to do the same.

Internals are pragmatic optimists. They see life's injustices, inequities, and negative circumstances, but consider every problem solvable. Internals recognize that it is unrealistic to expect massive change overnight, but that doesn't stop them from trying to effect change anyway. When they cannot quickly conquer the major goal they are working toward, they content themselves with incremental advances.

Likely Strengths

- ❏ Strong sense of duty
- ❏ Concerned and benevolent, with the energy to turn their empathy into action
- ❏ Compassionate advocates for the less fortunate
- ❏ Virtuous character
- ❏ Unlikely to compromise their values
- ❏ Make the effort to get involved and don't assume someone else will do it

Possible Pitfalls

Internals can become too narrow in their focus concerning the causes they love, and they may lose sight of the practical realities of running an organization. Because they are not motivated by money, they may become critical or judgmental of those who are. Internals can fall prey to self-righteousness or exhibit holier-than-thou behavior, believing themselves to be on the moral high ground. Focusing exclusively on the ideals that they support, Internals may lose the capacity to see other points of view. Internals may also run the risk of getting so absorbed in a cause that they neglect other relationships and responsibilities that are equally important.

Internals at Work

Internals like to know that their contributions are making a difference in their organization, their community, and the world at large. Job satisfaction is very important to them. Internals are passionate about doing work that is compatible with their values and want to express their values through their vocation. They believe their career should echo their beliefs and reflect what they deem important in life.

Internals have difficulty doing work that they philosophically disagree with. If an Internal believes in a cause, he or she will be extremely energized to work toward the goal. Internals believe that their job should be an expression of who they are, and that the result of their labor should somehow contribute to the betterment of mankind and the world.

The Internal wants a leader he can count on. A leader's commitment to integrity is more important than their natural talents, as far as the Internal is concerned. When Internals are in a leadership role, they have the ability to awaken hope in their followers. Internals believe that the best leaders are those dedicated to actions based on moral values and ethical standards.

Internals want the importance of their contribution to be apparent to others. They expect their supervisors to tell them that their part is appreciated. They want to enjoy the workplace, and a positive environment means a lot to them. However, their overriding wish is to do work that is significant and beneficial to others. Internals need to have a clear definition about the purpose of their work. They like to know the specific outcomes they are supposed to attain and why those outcomes are desirable. Then they want to visibly see the impact of their labor.

When Working with Internals

❏ Respect their beliefs, even if they differ from your own.

❏ Express appreciation for their contributions.

❏ Let them know that they are needed and valued.

❏ Show them how their part contributes to the whole in an indispensable way.

❏ Discuss the company's vision, values, and ethics and how they align with their personal beliefs.

❏ Demonstrate interest in their family, concerns, and passions.

❏ Allow Internals the opportunity to combine their values with their work.

Internals at Play

An Internal loves to feel that he or she has made a difference. For that reason, Internals often combine personal time with their love for charitable causes. It's not unusual to find them volunteering, training for marathons that benefit charity, or donating their time and talents in other ways. Internals love to champion causes. Contributing their time and knowledge and talent is part of how they find satisfaction at work and at home. Their desire to positively influence the world and help others is expressed in their social activities.

Internals in Relationships

Fidelity in personal relationships is very important to Internals. They have a very strong commitment to family and tend to be active in their communities. Internals expect their friends, family, and coworkers to act with integrity and keep their word. Internals are highly protective of those they love and become upset when people intentionally exploit or hurt others. Internals see a strong connection between doing the right thing, helping those who need help, and their own sense of well-being.

Resolving Conflict

Internals can become overly sensitive and feel insulted if they perceive that their positions are being ignored or overlooked. Because they have such definite opinions, Internals need to feel that their ideas have been heard, even if they are not implemented. Becoming offended by an injustice done to someone else can also be an issue for this motivational style. Internals are just as likely to be upset by the abuse of others as they are about their own mistreatment.

To resolve conflict with Internals, it is important that you hear them out. Give them the opportunity to put their grievance on the table and dissect it for you. Convey that you understand why they are upset and that it is justifiable for them to feel that way. This defuses their anger. Internals don't want you to simply calm them down or even to fix the problem—they want to know that you understand why they are irritated.

How Internals Influence Others

Internals influence others by taking ethical positions, making those viewpoints known, and adhering to them in word and deed.

Value to Organization

Internals are true believers. When they are sold on an organization or a cause, they are extremely loyal. Internals have the ability to focus a group on strategic outcomes. They can identify and articulate "why it matters," and create passion for projects among their peers.

Committed to principled action, Internals inspire a willingness to sacrifice. They are known for their wisdom as well as their intelligence. With a refusal to compromise on moral issues, they diligently keep their word and are virtually incorruptible in a leadership role. Internals look for ways to solve problems and create positive change. They have the ability to stay focused on the mission that brought the team together and will continually attend to the values shared by the organization.

De-Motivators

Internals can lose motivation when they feel powerless to change things, as well as by tasks that have no apparent positive outcomes. If they perceive that the bottom line is all that matters, they check out emotionally. They will work hard for a cause they believe in, but they will not work at all if they think the outcome will be negative, detrimental, or out of step with their personal ideals. Infringement on family or personal time can cause them to lose motivation, as does a disregard for values that they hold dear. Callous and prejudiced people who are only concerned about themselves anger Internals. If they distrust an individual or organization, Internals will become uncooperative.

Top Ten Motivators

1. Big vision for the future
2. Goals they feel are worthwhile and achievable
3. Private recognition

4. A sense of personal contribution
5. Receiving specific positive feedback and sincere appreciation
6. Corporate contribution to causes they are passionate about
7. Being rewarded with paid time off
8. Knowing that their work matters
9. Creating positive solutions
10. Righting injustice and helping the helpless

Awards for Internals

Today's workforce is ravenous for appreciation and positive recognition, but few feel they are getting it. Research shows that employees are primarily motivated by financial incentives and will significantly improve their performance in order to gain monetary awards. Internals, however, can see motivating employees with money as manipulative and may not be enticed by such propositions. Internals are more likely to be motivated to improve their performance through the use of non-monetary awards. For Internals, acknowledgment of their efforts produces organizational loyalty and job satisfaction. Here are some suggestions for low-cost/high-yield incentives that you can give Internals to recognize their contributions:

1. Flexible work hours
2. Freedom to implement their ideas
3. A nice place to take a mental break: a game room, a reading room, an inviting break room, a picnic table under a shady tree, etc.
4. Mementos or small, meaningful gifts that reflect their interests
5. A handwritten note of appreciation from their superior
6. Being recognized as Employee of the Month in a low-key rather than overstated way

7. Bigger role in decision making

8. A friendly, no-agenda lunch with the boss

9. Additional vacation time

10. Gift card to a favorite store

11. An article in the company newsletter about their contribution

12. Specific positive verbal feedback

13. Heartfelt recognition at departmental meetings

14. Professional portrait of the employee and their family

15. An occasional stop by their office or workstation for a light, informal chat

Advice for Internals

Don't be judgmental or harsh toward people who don't share your views. You are compassionate, but are you tolerant? Learn how to genuinely appreciate and unconditionally accept others, especially those with different lifestyles and ideologies. Make time for exercise, recreation, beauty, art, the enjoyment of nature, listening to music, and just doing nothing. Don't neglect yourself in your efforts to save the world.

FREE BONUS #9
Exclusive Celebrity Article—"The Four Essential
Characteristics of Inspired Leaders" by Rev. Billy Graham
(Priceless value)

Managers do things right. Leaders do the right thing. *Inspired* leaders do the right thing for the right reasons. In this exclusive article, Rev. Billy Graham shows you how to conquer the challenges of your world and leave a legacy of hope that will follow you into the future.

Why Externals Succeed
Financially

"Winners, I am convinced, imagine their dreams first.
They want it with all their heart and expect it to come true.
There is, I believe, no other way to live."

—JOE MONTANA

Joe Montana has a Super Bowl ring for each finger of his passing hand. He went to the Super Bowl four times, and four times he walked away with the trophy. From the age of eight, Joe dreamed of being a football star—and winning just added fuel to the fire. From Little League, to Notre Dame, to three-time Super Bowl MVP, Joe's fearless play is legendary.

Nicknamed "Joe Cool" for his unflappable composure in clutch situations, Montana was the master of late-game comebacks. He possessed an almost mythical calm in the midst of chaos. Joe led his teams to 31 fourth-quarter come-from-behind wins during his career.

Take, for example, the 1989 Super Bowl against the Cincinnati Bengals. Joe's San Francisco 49ers were down by three points with 3:20 left on the clock. Many QBs in that situation might ratchet into full-throttle panic, but not Joe. He casually turned to tackle Harris Barton in the huddle and said, "There, in the stands, standing near the exit ramp—isn't that John Candy?" It was a casual but deliberate effort to cut the tension of the moment. His eyes may have been in the stands, but believe me, his head was in the game. Joe went on to coolly complete eight of nine passes, moving the ball 92 yards down the field, and throwing the winning touchdown with 34 seconds to spare.

When Joe was enshrined in the Football Hall of Fame in 2000, Hall of Fame coach John Madden commented, "We say, 'He's the greatest quarterback I ever saw,' or 'He's the greatest quarterback this and that.' I say it with no disclaimers: This guy is the greatest quarterback who ever played."

Joe's extraordinary determination in part comes from the fact that he has an External Award system. Some of the most astute and successful people in sports, business, and entertainment are what I call Externals. They are high-intensity individuals who love to win. Prized by employers for their ability to generate revenues, Externals understand how to win, whatever the game.

Don't make the common mistake of thinking that Internals and Externals are complete opposites. They're not. Internals are *primarily* motivated by contribution, but financial compensation is still important to them. Externals are *primarily* motivated by the opportunity to succeed, but contribution is also important to them. Externals want to help others and be involved in great causes. They, too, want to leave a legacy. However, it is tangible benefits and material awards that make Externals feel valued and esteemed.

Winning trophies, achieving promotions, and higher salaries are quantifiable measures of success for the External. It lets them know how they are doing now and provides a gauge for future achievement. But remember, award systems are not a measure of character. Awards are simply motivational factors that make people feel valued. Although Internals are motivated by contribution, Externals tend to be just as kind, compassionate, and philanthropic as Internals.

The Motivational Value of Money

We cannot talk about motivation without talking about money. Is pay linked to performance? Will greater benefits secure greater accomplishments? Does money motivate employees?

The short answer: Yes.

The long answer: If you are an employer, you may not like it, but yes, it's the absolute truth. Money is a powerful motivator. All employees, whether they are Internal or External, are motivated by compensation. Internals are not predominantly money-motivated, but pay is still important to them. And when adequate compensation programs are not in place, it will de-motivate employees of every motivational type. Studies show that almost everyone is motivated by money to some degree.

- In a national survey of 2,500 employees, 91 percent said that if their company would share its success with its employees when organizational goals were achieved, they would be more motivated to help the company succeed.[1]
- In a survey of more than 1,500 compensation professionals, various types of monetary reward systems were found to have a "positive" or "very positive" impact on performance in 66 to 89 percent of the companies using techniques such as individual incentives, small-group incentives, profit sharing, and lump-sum bonuses.[2]
- According to a national survey of 1,200 randomly selected U.S. employees across many different types and sizes of companies, 54 percent

of employees rated direct financial compensation as "very important" or "extremely important" to motivation. When isolated by age group, Gen X and Gen Y were no different from baby boomers. There was no statistically significant difference in their responses.[3]

- A study was done of 663 companies, covering 1.3 million employees, with performance-reward compensation plans. This study sampled a broad section of the workforce of each company, not just managers and salespeople. The study found that at the median, organizations earned $2.34 for every dollar they spent on compensation, amounting to a net return on plan investment of approximately 134 percent.[4]

In the movie *Jerry Maguire,* Tom Cruise plays the title character, a sports agent who is fired from a prestigious management firm. In one of the film's most memorable scenes, Jerry's client Rod Tidwell, played by Cuba Gooding, Jr., tells Jerry that he will keep him as his agent rather than go with Jerry's competitor, Bob Sugar. The phone exchange between Jerry and Rod is a great illustration of the External's motivation.

Rod Tidwell: This is what I'm gonna do for you: God bless you, Jerry. But what you gonna do for me, Jerry?

Jerry Maguire: Yeah, what can I do for you, Rod? You just tell me. What can I do for you?

Rod Tidwell: It's something very personal, a very important thing. . . . It's a family motto. Are you ready, Jerry? I wanna make sure you're ready, brother. Here it is: Show me the money. SHOW . . . ME . . . THE . . . MONEY! Jerry, it is such a pleasure to say that! Say it with me one time, Jerry.

Jerry Maguire: Show you the money.

Rod Tidwell: No! Not show you! Show ME the money. . . . I want you to say it, brother, with meaning! Hey, I got Bob Sugar on the other line. I bet you he can say it. . . .

Jerry Maguire: No, no, no. Show me the money!

Rod Tidwell: I need to feel you, Jerry!

Jerry Maguire: Show me the money! SHOW ME THE MONEY!

Temperament

Externals are goal-oriented and energetic. They want to be rewarded in tangible, material ways, but they expect to work hard to achieve their compensation. They enjoy spending time with influential people and respect the opinions of high achievers. Externals work hard and play hard. They are quick to spot the latest trends and they want to have it all.

Externals love to play on the winning team. They thrive on recognition and reward, and will honor others in the same way. In leadership roles, they are generous to their high-level performers. Externals like the attention that comes with success and the respect that accompanies authority. They enjoy being in positions where they can call the shots and run the show. Power and influence make them come alive.

The Success-Oriented External

For more than four decades, Michael Eisner has been a leader in the entertainment industry. His career began at ABC, where he helped take the network from No. 3 to No. 1 in prime time, daytime, and children's television with such landmark shows as *Happy Days*, *Barney Miller*, and *Roots*.

Later, as president of Paramount Pictures, he led the studio to first place in the box office and profitability for both theatrical movies and network television production. After that, Eisner spent twenty-one years as chairman and CEO of The Walt Disney Company, transforming it into a global media empire valued at $60 billion.

Recently, I had the privilege of hosting Michael at one of our GET MOTIVATED Seminars. I was impressed with his charming, down-to-earth likability and by his aptitude for detail—particularly when it came to numbers and finance. In his entertaining and information-packed speech he gave several clues about his External Award system. For example, he told the following story about one of his projects:

> Let me tell you about a film I'm sure you're all familiar with, *Raiders of the Lost Ark*. Of course, it's now a classic, but we didn't know that when we green-lit it during my tenure at Paramount. Believe it or not, every other studio passed on the project because the idea of a globe-trotting archaeologist sounded like it would result in the most expensive film in history. But Steven Spielberg and George Lucas assured us they could deliver the picture within a surprisingly modest financial box. We set a budget that was pretty tight, and Steven and George kept their end of the bargain.
>
> One day, Harrison Ford had—how do I put this gently?—digestive problems, which delayed filming. He was supposed to do one more elaborate fight scene with the guy with the big sword, but he was feeling lousy and wanted to get back to his room. This would have meant another day of filming, adding significant costs to the production. So it was decided to just have Harrison shoot the guy with a gun so everybody could go home and the movie could stay on budget. Not only did we save money on this scene, but it turned out better than if Steven—with our encouragement—hadn't micromanaged the project and instead had simply spent the extra money to do it as it was initially written. As you can see, creativity can actually flourish within sensible financial limitations.
>
> And the opposite can certainly be the case. Any number of megabudget films have been megaflops because they attempted to substitute greater capital expenditure for creativity. This rarely

works. One such example, years back, was the film *Raise the Titanic*. After the experience, producer Lew Grade concluded, "It would have been cheaper to lower the Atlantic."

The audience was spellbound by Eisner's speech. I was particularly struck by his dexterity at knitting numbers through the fabric of his message. Among the stats that he rattled off:

❑ "In 1996, we bought CapCities/ABC, which included the ESPN sports cable network. Analysts today estimate that ESPN alone is worth twice what we paid for the entire CapCities/ABC acquisition."

❑ "We built thirty-two Disney hotels with more than 30,000 rooms . . . and I insisted that there be lights that are actually bright enough to read by, unlike the twenty-five-watt bulbs that some hotels seem to favor."

❑ "Our team managed to find singers in every language who had precisely the right vocal quality to serve the dramatic needs of the film. Thanks in part to this micromanagement, *The Lion King* grossed $455 million outside the United States, a full $125 million more than it did in the U.S."

❑ "When the first *Pirates* film was proposed, many people were very concerned it would fail. Their opinion was based on the fact that there had not been a successful pirate-themed film in decades. Of course, it proved to be a risk well worth taking, as the three *Pirates of the Caribbean* films have grossed more than $2.5 billion worldwide."

It is precisely this mastery over detail, fiscal responsibility, and management that made Michael Eisner one of the most respected, successful CEOs in history. This is also why there is fierce competition for highly talented Externals in the marketplace. They are go-getters who pay attention to the bottom line.

EXTERNALS IN THEIR OWN WORDS

"Every day, I get up and look through the Forbes list of the richest people in America. If I'm not there, I go to work."
—Robert Orben

"As a player, it says everything about you if you made the Hall of Fame. But then again, boy . . . there's something about winning a Super Bowl."
—Terry Bradshaw

"Power is the ultimate aphrodisiac."
—Henry Kissinger

"Everyone in showbiz is driven by ego, so how do you go from having loads of fame to working at 7-Eleven? You can't do it!"
—Ryan Seacrest

"The woman who can create her own job is the woman who will win fame and fortune."
—Amelia Earhart

"It's a kind of spiritual snobbery that makes people think they can be happy without money."
—Albert Camus

"Almost anyone can be an author; the business is to collect money and fame from this state of being."
—A. A. Milne

"Money is better than poverty, if only for financial reasons."
—Woody Allen

"Fame is like a VIP pass wherever you want to go."
—Leonardo DiCaprio

"If winning isn't everything, why do they keep score?"
—Vince Lombardi

*"I just want the money and the fame and the adoration.
I don't want any of the other stuff."*
—Matthew Broderick

*"Winning is the most important thing in my life, after breathing.
Breathing first, winning next."*
—George Steinbrenner

*"I always knew I was going to be rich.
I don't think I ever doubted it for a minute."*
—Warren Buffett

Communication Style

Externals tend to be forthcoming and candid. They want to communicate skillfully to ensure clarity. They are usually comfortable and confident in their ability to express themselves. But many Externals need to work on their listening skills. They may put forth more effort trying to be understood than they do listening to what others have to say.

Externals believe that credit should be given where credit is due. They are happy to recognize others when it is deserved, and they feel there is nothing wrong with receiving recognition when they have earned it. In general, Externals relish praise; it energizes them and satisfies their desire to be acknowledged for their efforts.

When Communicating with Externals

❑ Highlight the benefits—show them what is to be gained organizationally and personally.

❑ Soon after an accomplishment, compliment them.

❑ Single them out for deserved recognition in the presence of their peers.

❑ Offer a big prize for difficult challenges.

❑ Every chance you get, affirm them for their special talents and positive contributions.

Cognitive Process

Externals are bottom-line thinkers. They want to know the probable outcome before they invest time and energy in an endeavor. Tell them they can't do something and they'll prove you wrong just to prove the point. Externals are performers—they get the job done, motivated by the belief that their achievements will be recognized and rewarded. The feeling of accomplishment is tied to the External's identity. Externals see themselves as achievers. It's not just what they do; it's who they are.

Counting tangible assets as a way of measuring their success, Externals are highly motivated by compensation and perks. They value success and admire people who have achieved it. Externals want the opportunity to be promoted and to influence decision making. They like to express their creative ideas through their work and to be in a position to run the show. Externals are in a rush to win—the sooner the better. The bigger the prize, the quicker they want to claim it. They put a lot of effort into their endeavors and need to receive acknowledgment for the work they do.

Likely Strengths

- ❏ Energized by challenge
- ❏ Enterprising and resourceful
- ❏ Goal-oriented
- ❏ Unwilling to give up if there is a big upside benefit
- ❏ Determined and diligent
- ❏ Aspire to be the best

Possible Pitfalls

Externals can be very high-maintenance. If something goes unnoticed or unrewarded, it discourages them. Their desire for continual affirmation can wear on those they work and live with. If high-performing Externals are not recognized by their organization for the significance of their contribution, they will not be around for long. They will begin to look for other opportunities. Externals also have a tendency to become dissatisfied when they choose to do work that they don't enjoy simply because it pays them more.

Externals love accolades and can easily slip into the "hero" role. When they are succeeding, Externals risk feeling invincible and need to do regular reality checks to keep their egos under control. They may become arrogant and elevate their own achievements over those of their co-contributors. With an eye on the prize, Externals can be too determined to win and may ignore signs to slow down or back off. It is difficult for Externals to admit defeat. They can be very focused and driven in their quest to advance, even at the expense of their health, time for recreation, and relationships.

Externals at Work

Externals need opportunities to advance in their careers. If those opportunities evaporate, so does their motivation. They desire to have a significant role in their organizations, along with increasing influence. Externals want their special abilities to be recognized and validated by their superiors. They like their bosses to recognize their accomplishments and want their coworkers to be aware of how well they do their jobs.

As long as Externals are there at the end to see the result and reap the reward, they don't mind an uphill struggle or difficult assignment. They enjoy having the sense of triumph at the completion of every day. Hardworking and ambitious, Externals like knowing that they are doing a good job and want the impact of their role on organizational goals to be noticed.

Externals want to work in an environment where success is celebrated. They expect their ideas and opinions to be taken into account by their superiors. They also want easy access to the people, tools, and materials they need to get the job done.

The main reason Externals do their job is to make a splash, get noticed, excel, and prosper. They do not have a "just-doing-my-job" mentality. Years of faithfully executing the same task does not appeal to them. They want to grow in knowledge and responsibility. Externals expect their job to supply opportunities for increased authority, prestige, benefits, and compensation. In short, they want to be rewarded for their success by an increase in either pay or status, but preferably both.

When Working with Externals
- ❏ Recognize their achievements and praise them in public.
- ❏ Link challenging goals to enticing incentives.
- ❏ Ask for their input on supervisory matters.

❑ Give regular performance feedback.

❑ Reward achievement in tangible ways.

❑ Make sure they understand their compensation plans and how they can get ahead in the organization.

❑ Give them opportunities to lead.

Externals at Play

Physical surroundings and comforts are important to Externals. They appreciate the finer things in life. After work, they want to enjoy family and friends, along with the benefits that their work has afforded them. They splurge to celebrate their own successes and the achievements of those they love. Fine dining, great seats at sporting events, shopping, and resort vacations are among the recreational activities that Externals enjoy.

Large-scale productions, displays of splendor, and excellence in execution inspire Externals. They are stimulated by grandeur, whether it is a magnificent example of architecture, a breathtaking panorama of nature, or a lavish display of pageantry. Externals love to see feats of strength and record-breaking wins. Over-the-top achievement energizes them both at work and at play.

Externals in Relationships

Externals want to make sure that their family is well provided for and enjoy making life comfortable for those they care about. Externals need to be admired and respected. They like people to be impressed by their performance. Externals try to woo potential love interests with their charm, charisma, status, and success. They want a mate who will laugh at their jokes, esteem their abilities, and affirm their positive qualities. Externals tend to be visual and are attracted to attractive people. What's on the inside matters, but what's on the outside is what grabs their attention.

Resolving Conflict

Externals are prone to take a firm stand when confronted. They are people who know what they want and are determined to get it. They may be inclined to operate from a position of power, citing their superior skill or rank. When engaged in a dispute with an External, it is important to be respectful, even if you are upset. Externals are sensitive to how they are perceived by others and want to be seen in the best light possible.

To defuse anger, point out their positive traits: "I've always known you to be a reasonable, fair-minded person with an extraordinary ability to relate to others." Be open to compromise. Ask what is most important to the External and what solutions might satisfy him or her. Then talk about how they can get the outcome they desire.

How Externals Influence Others

Externals influence others by their passion for excellence, determination to win, and by creating a climate conducive to high productivity.

Value to Organization

Properly motivated, Externals raise the bar in any organization. Their example motivates the rest of the team and inspires others to improve performance. At their best, Externals are energized achievers whose resolute determination and goal-oriented focus increase corporate profitability.

De-Motivators

Work for work's sake does not appeal to Externals. They tend to lose motivation in any mission without commission. Tasks without obvious rewards hold little interest for Externals. If they cannot see the benefit—or worse yet, if it seems to them that a loss will occur—they become disengaged.

Top Ten Motivators

1. Monetary compensation
2. Individual recognition from superiors
3. Promotion or opportunity for advancement
4. Special privileges
5. Incentive plans to spur production
6. Freedom from controls and supervision
7. Perks such as paid vacations
8. Bonuses
9. Awards, plaques, and trophies commemorating high achievement
10. Public acknowledgment

Awards for Externals

Money is never an effective substitute for good management, but incentive plans can be wonderful motivators for both External and Internal employees. In an environment of limited resources, you may not be able to provide everything Externals want (let's face it, they want it all). But if you are unable to give a bigger paycheck or promotion to your high-performing External, look for other ways to enrich him or her. Externals want monetary and positional advancement, not for its own sake but because it is a clear indicator of success. It proves to them, and others, that they are winners. If you can't give Externals more money, give them other things that they really want: status, respect, and public acknowledgment. Here are some ways that you can recognize and reward Externals:

1. More prestigious title
2. Leadership opportunities that allow them to flex their managerial muscles
3. Office with a view
4. Invitation to participate in meetings or meals with the executive team
5. Public verbal recognition, preferably accompanied with a gift or award
6. Opportunities for advancement
7. Profit sharing, stock options, or warrants
8. Project- or performance-based bonuses
9. Reserved parking space
10. Child-care subsidies
11. Tuition reimbursements
12. Premium-seat tickets to sporting events
13. Gadgets: the latest and greatest cell phone, laptop, or PDA
14. Luxury items, such as an engraved Mont Blanc pen
15. Concierge service to pick up their dry cleaning, run errands, buy gifts, etc.

Advice for Externals

You are talented, and you know it. But make sure that you share the credit. Ask coworkers for feedback and be willing to let others challenge your ideas. Don't put off your personal life in pursuit of your career goals. Recognize your limitations and don't ignore the signs of burnout. Make time for your partner and remember how quickly children grow up.

FREE BONUS #10

One-on-One Telephone Coaching Session with One of Tamara's Financial Success Coaches. ($199 value)

With debt soaring, savings plummeting, the housing market tanking, the economy globalizing, and boomers almost completely unprepared for retirement, the need for financial triage has never been more urgent. So whether you're just starting out in life, or are on the home stretch to retirement, you need the wisdom and solid counsel that a financial coach can bring. In your next book bonus, you will create a personalized success blueprint with one of our Financial Success coaches.

PART THREE

HOW TO RAISE POSITIVE, SELF-MOTIVATED CHILDREN

Tips and Techniques for
Motivating Young Children

re you tired of nagging your children to get them to pick up
after themselves? Weary of pestering them to do homework? Are you sick of saying the same things over and over
and over again? Would you like to know the secrets of raising self-
motivated children? If so, Part Three of this book is for you.

If you are a parent, I believe this section alone is worth the price of
the entire book. The following pages are going to transform your life
and your children's lives. I so firmly believe this that I am going to ask
you to do me a favor. If, after reading this section, you feel the way I do,
will you please share this book with other parents and teachers? As
more adults use this information, more children will benefit.

The following few chapters address the five phases of childhood and
the different motivators that are needed at each of these stages:

❑ Infants to Toddlers (birth to age 3)
❑ Early Childhood (ages 4–11)
❑ Students (pre-K to college)
❑ Teens (ages 12–19)
❑ Young Adults (ages 20–25)

In this and the following few chapters, I will take you phase by phase through the life of a child. In this chapter, you will learn how to motivate children in the early stages of childhood, from birth through age eleven. Chapter 13 will show you how to inspire academic excellence in your children, from preschool to grad school. Then, in Chapter 14, we will cover the keys to motivating teenagers and young adults.

As we travel through the various phases of childhood, I will point out the top parental priorities during each stage. I will also address the most pressing problems related to each phase of childhood. For example, here are the four most common questions I hear from parents and teachers:

1. How can I help my children to do well in school?
2. How can I motivate my kids to be more cooperative and obedient?
3. How can I get my children to be responsible and help out around the house?
4. What is the most effective way to communicate with my kids?

In this section of the book, I will answer these questions and more. Of course, the basics never change. Children need love. They need affirmation and encouragement. They crave our time and attention. They need to play and have fun. Kids have a spiritual core and desire moral guidance. They need affection, stability, and tranquillity in the home. Parents and teachers must *be there* for children—not just physically, but also emotionally.

Children generally fall into two different camps—those who are compliant (Connectors) and those who are inclined to test the limits (Producers). As I explained in Chapter 1, I have one of each. My firstborn, Zack, is fifteen. His younger brother, Blaize, is ten. Blaize is content, easygoing, and cooperative. At heart, he wants to please. On the rare occasion when I need to correct Blaize, all I have to do is say, "Son, you need to obey Mom," and he does. He has an obedient spirit. Any nitwit could parent my younger son. Zack, however, as I described earlier, is a challenge—an amazing, wonderful, witty challenge. In this section of the book, I want to address the challenges of motivating children, and I will primarily use Zack to help illustrate this.

Phase One: Infants to Toddlers (Birth to Age 3)

OUR JOB: Protect them, nurture them, teach them civility, and keep them from killing themselves.

Just hours after giving birth, I was stunned to discover that my husband and I were being allowed to bring our firstborn home. I said to the nurse, "That's it? We just diaper and dress the infant—and then we leave? Don't we need a license or a parenting class or something?" She smiled and said, "No. Just keep him from killing himself. Protect him from sticking beans in his ears, pennies in his mouth, and ballpoint pens up his nose. Keep him from falling down the stairs and investigating electrical outlets with metal objects."

After the initial joy, delirium, shock, and awe wear off, a parent's primary questions during this phase spring from a place of deep, unimaginable exhaustion.

YOUR QUESTIONS: What have I done? Will it get easier? Will it ever end?
THE ANSWERS: Yes, it will get easier. But no, it will never end.

Once you acclimate to sleep deprivation, you learn how to haul around the sixty-five pounds of indispensable equipment needed to care for an eight-pound infant and go for days on end without a shower. You learn to choose your clothes based on patterns that will best blend with spit-up. But that's just the beginning.

Protection and Correction

During the first stage of childhood, our main responsibilities are to protect and correct. If you want to enter a whole new realm of parental paranoia, log on to www.familywatchdog.us/showmap.asp. Type in your address and you'll get the names, addresses, and photos of all the registered sex offenders in your neighborhood. I did a search from my home using a three-mile radius and found 220 pedophiles! And these are just the registered ones. That doesn't include the ones who have not yet been caught or convicted. My point: We need to keep a watchful eye on our kids at every stage, and especially when they are too young to communicate. First and foremost, our job as parents is to protect our children.

Next, we must instruct our offspring so that they evolve from wild, tantrum-prone brats who appear to have been raised by wolves into charming children who may be seen in public without apology. Which brings me to my next motivational lesson, *boundaries*. Children need limits. Limits equal love.

When my husband and I built our house, there was a period of about a week when there were no rails on the upstairs balcony. Our children begged to go out on the balcony and promised us that they would not venture to the edge. Of course, we said no. In the same way we would not permit our children to play on a balcony without rails, we must not allow them to go through life without boundaries. Rules are like the rails on a balcony. They provide safety for children. Boundaries make them feel loved, secure, and protected.

The word *No,* so beautiful in its simplicity, is a word that you must never be afraid to say to your children. When my son Blaize was about three years old, we were shopping in Wal-Mart. As we stood in the checkout line, we observed a mother and her preschool son have a squabble about a toy that the child wanted. The mother told the boy that he couldn't have the toy. The child threw himself on the floor and began shrieking like he'd been poked in the eye with a sharp stick, kicking his feet and beating his fists on the ground. The mother was embarrassed. My son was perplexed.

Finally, Blaize asked me, "Mommy, what's wrong with that boy?"

"He's having a temper tantrum."

"What's that?" Blaize asked.

"It's when a child screams and yells to try and get his way."

Blaize processed that for a moment and then said, "That child needs consequences."

At this point, to calm him down, the mother of the wailing toddler told him she would buy him the toy.

"Yes," I said. "He needs consequences, and so does his mom."

Sadly, the little boy that mother was indulging *is* her consequence. A three-year-old having a tantrum is one thing. That same child having a tantrum at thirteen is another thing entirely. Remember this, because it's true about every relationship you will ever have: **Whatever you tolerate you will get more of.**

If you don't like a behavior, you must not tolerate it. Babies cry and toddlers throw tantrums. That is normal behavior in the Infant-Toddler Phase. But parents must act like parents and have the courage to patiently correct and lovingly discipline their children—at every stage.

When Zack was about three years old and could not get his way, he had a favorite declaration that he would proclaim with passionate indignation:

"*YOU* are not making me happy!"

"It's not my job to make you happy," I would reply. "It's my job to love and protect you. I am responsible for teaching you to be a kind, moral person and a good, law-abiding citizen. And you know what? I think I'm doing a great job! You're turning into a fine young man."

After hearing the same answer dozens of times, Zack stopped expecting me to make him happy. Now, at this point, you may think that I've not taught you a single thing about how to motivate children. And you're right. What I've done so far is encourage you to be a motivated parent. Motivated parents produce motivated children.

I've got a spoonful of preventative medicine to offer you: Teach your young children how to honor others, submit to authority, follow rules, and be responsible, polite, kind, generous, and loving. Then, later on in life, you won't have to motivate them to speak respectfully to authority figures, stop stealing and cheating, get off drugs, be chaste, work hard in school, get a good job, be reliable, and provide for their own families. Again—*motivated parents produce motivated children.*

RECOMMENDED RESOURCES

The resources that I am going to recommend at the conclusion of each section represent the best information from the thousands of books, videos, audios, and tools that I have personally reviewed and tested. In my opinion, the most helpful parenting books on the market have been written by the following five authors: Pediatrician Dr. William Sears and his wife, Martha, who are the parents of eight children; child psychologist Dr. James Dobson; and parenting experts Gary and Anne Marie Ezzo. Among the five of them, they've written more than a hundred books.

The Ezzos have very helpful information on training young children to be polite and well-mannered. Using their materials, I taught both of my children basic sign language so that they could communicate before they were old enough to speak. Our babies learned how to say *please, thank you, more, food, drink,* and other simple words in sign language. The authors I've recommended have books to address every possible parenting dilemma, from potty training to raising strong-willed children to the different methods needed to raise a boy or a girl. These authors produce books that are well researched, well written, and packed with practical information.

Phase Two: Early Childhood (Ages 4–11)

OUR JOB: Enjoy them, affirm them, and build friendship for the upcoming (potentially turbulent) teen years.

The easiest time to be a parent is when children are between the ages of four and eleven. The baby phase is over. Your children can dress themselves and are less dependent on you to physically care for them. Now you get an eight-year reprieve to prepare for the teen years. This is your last chance to cuddle your kids and hold them close, to play with them and make memories before the challenges of the Teen Phase begin.

YOUR QUESTION: How do I motivate my children to help around the house and clean their rooms?

THE ANSWER: I'm going to give you some resources to help you. But first, let's focus on the most important thing—play!

I'm convinced that the two primary motivators in the Early Childhood Phase are play and sugar. Kids can't seem to get enough of either one. Because we have two sons in our house, play revolves around combat: foam-sword duels, light-saber battles, Silly String fights, Nerf gun wars, rubber-ball brawls . . . you name it. Boys can turn any toy into a weapon.

What should you do during the Early Childhood Phase?

1. Play with your kids
2. Help your children discover their talents
3. Celebrate their uniqueness
4. Provide stability
5. Make memories

One of the gifts of parenthood is that we get to experience the joys of childhood again through our children. We can watch ants, blow bubbles, make snow angels, finger-paint, play baseball, and do all kinds of wonderful kid stuff. Enter into the fun and make time to play with your children.

Celebrate your children's strengths.
Help your children find their innate talents. Expose them to a variety of sports, arts, educational experiences, and bodies of knowledge. When you recognize an area of interest, encourage their participation. Help them hone their gifts. Constantly affirm their character qualities, talents, and abilities. Don't rush to rescue your children from every frustrating experience. Let them work through the frustration and figure out solutions for themselves. Knowing that they can find answers will help build their self-confidence.

Provide stability.
Ensure that there is structure and harmony in your home. Don't argue in front of your children. In my home, we do not watch television shows where a family is depicted arguing or where children speak disrespect-

fully to adults. "Oh, Tamara, that's extreme," you might say. Okay, I'm extreme. But there is peace in my home. My children speak respectfully to adults. They don't call each other names or put each other down.

Eat dinner together as a family.

According to a growing body of research, including studies from Harvard and Columbia Universities, children who eat with their families at least five times a week get better grades in school and are much less likely to abuse substances. Teenagers having family dinners five or more times a week were 42 percent less likely to drink alcohol, 59 percent less likely to smoke cigarettes, and 66 percent less likely to try marijuana. Frequent family meals are also associated with a lower incidence of depression and suicide, a lower likelihood of eating disorders among girls, and less teenage sexual activity.

I am well aware of the challenges of getting a family together for dinner. My children are involved in after-school sports. Both my husband and I work. I travel several times a month. It's not easy. But my husband and I make it a priority and we eat dinner together as a family at least five days a week.

Twice a week we have "Family Fun Night" following dinner. We eat dessert; read from books; talk about sports, news, and politics; and play board games with the kids. One of the more popular segments of Fun Night is called "Outrage of the Day," where family members are free to vent (usually with added embellishment) about their most frustrating experiences. Our children look forward to Family Fun Night and it is a great time for us to connect with them.

Write love notes.

From the time that my children were able to read, I've written them love notes. Sometimes I leave a little card on their pillow or tuck a note of encouragement into their lunchbox. Often they are just a few sentences, such as the following:

"You studied hard and you're going to do great on your exam!"

"I'm proud of you! You're a wonderful son!"

"I have a surprise for you when you come home from school today. . . . We're going bowling!"

I created a line drawing of myself and sign my notes with this:

As my children got older, around the age of eight, I began writing one-page letters to commemorate very special accomplishments. My children treasure these letters and save them. They are happy for days after getting one. At the end of Chapter 13, I'm going to share a few of these letters with you as examples. I encourage you to write notes to your children. It is a meaningful and memorable way to affirm how much you love them.

Create memories.

Bake cookies, visit the county fair, go on bike rides, and enjoy picnics and sports together. Celebrate family traditions, prepare family recipes, and incorporate religious customs in your home. Annual traditions are important to children. Make valentines, decorate gingerbread houses, play the Dreidel game, dye Easter eggs . . . all of these rituals are important to kids.

In our home, when we notice a significant improvement in the grades, attitudes, or behavior of our children we have a "Next Level Celebration." We put a "congratulations" banner on the wall, wear tall hats, and make the biggest stack of chocolate-chip pancakes you've ever seen!

RECOMMENDED RESOURCES

We all know the potential dangers of sexual predators and online pornography. Filtering software adds an additional layer of defense. It gives you the ability to control content, block Web sites, filter e-mail, block pop-ups, and monitor chat rooms. Every computer in your home should have filtering capabilities. I recommend that you go online and look at comparison reviews of the latest software. Pick one and install it.

The other tool I recommend can be found online at www.easychild. com. This is a system that rewards positive behaviors and eliminates negative ones. Children earn their privileges based on how many points they accumulate each week. In less than an hour, you can customize the system for your family. After that, it takes just fifteen minutes a week. Children learn that when they do what's expected they get privileges, and when they don't do what's expected they don't get privileges. In about three weeks' time, children change their strategy from arguing to get what they want to looking for ways to earn it. You can also use the built-in allowance feature to calculate earned allowance by assigning a monetary value to each point.

Now let's turn our attention to inspiring a love of learning in children. At a time when rock stars, actors, and athletes are our children's heroes, it's hard to convince kids that education is the real key to success. But there are proven ways that parents and teachers can motivate their children to enjoy school, work hard (by their own initiative), and achieve outstanding academic success. That's the subject of Chapter 12.

FREE BONUS #11

**Exclusive Celebrity Article—"9 Principles for
Better Parenting" by Pat Williams, Senior Vice President
of the NBA Orlando Magic and father of 19 children.
(Priceless value)**

Yes, *19* children—that's not a typo, and it's not even the most amazing part. Fourteen were adopted from other nations, and 16 of them were teenagers *at the same time*. Yet Pat Williams lived to tell about it.... Believe me, you're going to want to read what he has to say!

Keys to Helping Kids Achieve
Academic Success

Did you know that 80 percent of people, following high school or college graduation, will never buy and read another book again—*for the rest of their lives?* I find that statistic tragic. It suggests that we have taught kids to hate education. I would much rather my children gain a love of learning at school, rather than merely accumulate information.

As parents and teachers, our job is to help our children develop enthusiasm for education and the skills they need for academic achievement. The good news is that it's never too early or too late to start. How can you motivate your children to study, do their homework, and get good grades? In this chapter, I am going to give you five keys that will unlock scholastic success for your children.

I am both a parent and a teacher. I've taught children of all ages, from prekindergarten to graduate students, and now teach teachers and educators around the world. I serve as a visiting professor at universities and colleges all over the country. As a former dropout with an eighth-grade education, I am humbled by this honor. Over the years, I've gone on to earn undergraduate and graduate degrees, and I am grateful for the opportunity to contribute to our educational system.

I've had the pleasure to work with public and private school teachers, training them how to motivate their students. The insights I am going to reveal in this chapter are based on that experience. In my work with teachers and parents, I've picked up on a shared concern: It is an underlying sense of guilt. Fathers feel bad that they are not spending more time with their children. Working mothers suspect that they are shortchanging their kids. Stay-at-home moms confess that they struggle with endless responsibilities that leave them depleted. Teachers also feel overwhelmed and ill-equipped.

In the classroom, unmotivated students are costing America untold millions of dollars, lost time, and opportunity. Teachers commonly complain that students are not interested in school, are unmotivated to learn, and are unwilling to do what teachers expect of them. Experts say that about half of the students in classrooms do not make a consistent effort to learn. The toll this is taking on teachers—and the more motivated students—is enormous. However, there is hope. Using the principles of Motivational DNA, we can motivate children to improve their performance at school, at home, and in every aspect of their lives.

Key #1: Appeal to Your Child's Motivational DNA

The teachers I have worked with report over and over again that when they use Motivational DNA in the classroom, attention and grades dramatically improve. Why? Motivational DNA is a student-based approach that cultivates a love of learning, rather than a curriculum-honoring approach that force-feeds students a set of facts. The head-master of one of the most respected private schools in the country recently told me, "The two challenges teachers constantly cite with their students are motivation and discipline. Motivational DNA helps solve both of those problems."

A few months ago, one of Zack's teachers called, saying, "Mrs. Lowe, I'm having trouble with Zack; I may need you to get involved."

"Okay," I said. "Please tell me what's wrong."

"Well, Zack is disrupting the class," Mrs. Ford said. "Every time something funny pops into his head, he feels the need to blurt it out. The more his classmates laugh, the more he does it."

"Yes, I can see how that would be disruptive."

"When I correct him, he doesn't seem to care. He just ignores me. It's obvious he doesn't respect me."

"That is definitely a problem," I said. "Mrs. Ford, I'm happy to speak to Zack. However, I've done a lot of research on student mo-tivation and I've learned a few things about Zack that I think will help you."

I explained Zack's Motivational DNA type to Mrs. Ford and then I said, "If you are interested in conducting an experiment, I don't think you'll have any more problems with Zack."

"Okay, what should I do?"

"First of all, it's important to know that, at heart, Zack is a soldier. He enjoys a fight and doesn't back down easily. However, he will re-spect and obey his commanding officer if the commander *likes him* and *acknowledges his leadership abilities*. Those are the two secret ingredi-ents. Zack loves to conquer a challenge. You don't need to lower the bar for him. You can raise the bar and he'll hurdle it. Tell Zack that you really like and respect him. By the way, if you genuinely don't like Zack, he'll sense it. This will only work if you sincerely like him. Tell him what you admire about him. Next, tell him that it is clear to you that he is the class leader and that all of his peers look to him for direction. Tell him that you recognize he is the key to unlocking the potential of the whole group. Let him know that you are counting on him to set an example because the other kids will follow his lead. Then thank him for his maturity in hearing you out."

"All right, I'll try that."

"Thank you. Please call me if this doesn't resolve the situation."

I didn't hear a word from Mrs. Ford for weeks. Finally, curiosity got the better of me and I called her. "So, what happened?" I asked.

"I did what you said and Zack has been an angel ever since. You were right—in fact, the behavior and attention of the whole class dramatically improved. It's miraculous! However, I tried it with a couple of students in my other classes and it didn't work."

"That's because your other students have different Motivational DNA. The very thing that motivated Zack may serve to demotivate a student with a different motivational type. First, you must crack the students' codes. Once you do, I think you'll get terrific results."

At this point, I'd like to address the teachers, administrators, and educators reading this book. You are my heroes. Thank you for putting up with our children. Thank you for loving them, helping them, and teaching them. The impact you have on our children is enormous. A few words of affirmation from you, spoken in the hallway or written at the top of a paper, rock their world. It is a joy and privilege for me to contribute a tool that will help make your jobs easier.

Over the past five years, I've met with hundreds of educators to identify what award-winning teachers do to motivate their students. Here are the seven motivators that teachers themselves cite as most effective in the classroom:

1. Create a space for students to contribute.
2. Honor the students as individuals. Get to know and enjoy them.

3. Make it fun for students to come to school. Give them things to look forward to.

4. Establish structure. Make the rules known, along with the consequences of violating the rules. When consequences need to be implemented, enforce them, gently, without anger.

5. Identify and encourage each student's special abilities and talents.

6. Reward achievement through recognition, such as displaying the students' work.

7. Reward achievement through tangible awards, such as giving out candy to those who answer correctly during test preparation.

When I set out to discover the motivators that top teachers use, I had no idea that they would so closely correlate to my own research. Interestingly, all seven of the motivators listed above are elements of Motivational DNA. Teachers across the nation have taken the principles of Motivational DNA and incorporated them into their lessons with great success. Some of the innovative ways that they have utilized this information include having students who are Connectors work in teams, creating contests for students who are Producers, allowing students who are Variables to perform skits or songs, inviting students who are Stabilizers to tutor classmates for credit, and offering both Internal and External Awards to spur the performance of their students.

Key #2: Applaud Effort, Not Intelligence

One of the most interesting studies on student motivation that I've come across suggests that praising children for their *intelligence* has a negative impact on performance and leaves them poorly equipped to cope with failure. However, commending children for their *effort* makes them eager to learn more.

Claudia M. Mueller and Carol S. Dweck, research psychologists at Columbia University, studied 412 fifth-graders and found that praising children's intelligence, far from boosting their self-esteem, encourages them to embrace self-defeating behaviors such as worrying about failure and avoiding risks. These findings conflict with the common belief that praising children for their ability is likely to motivate them.

After being given easy problems from an IQ test, some of the children were praised for being smart, while others were praised for their effort. Next, the children in the study were given a choice between a challenging test and an easier test. Sixty percent of the children who had been praised for being smart chose the easy test, whereas ninety percent who had been praised for their effort picked the difficult one.

Later, when all the children took a difficult test, the intelligence-praised children were more likely to become frustrated and lose interest.

"The results were much stronger than we expected," said Dr. Dweck. "When children are taught the value of concentrating, strategizing, and working hard when dealing with academic challenges, this encourages them to sustain their motivation, performance, and self-esteem."

Key #3: Parental Participation

Grades significantly improve when parents increase their involvement in the process. It pays to supervise during homework time, help your child with organization, communicate with teachers regularly, and review test material with your child before exams.

Show your children how to take legible notes using an outline format that categorizes the information in sections with titles, subtitles, and numbers. Teach them to listen for topics and write down supporting points of the main idea. Have them underline, circle, or mark the important points and details that will likely appear on tests.

Parental involvement sends a strong signal to your kids that education is a priority. Reading to your children also makes a difference, even in the teen years. Once your child enjoys reading, his or her grades will automatically improve in all subjects.

Key #4: Link Privileges to Grades

Good grades should be celebrated and rewarded. Earning privileges like weekend outings, sleepovers, and extracurricular activities can be powerful motivators for children. When our son wanted to play football in seventh grade, we told him it was conditional on his ability to get on the honor roll. His grades instantaneously shot up and we haven't seen a C on his report card in years! Cell phones, computer time, video games, later bedtime, extra desserts, and use of the family car (for older teens) can all be linked to grades. If a child has to earn his or her privileges through good grades, believe me, grades will improve.

Key #5: Teach Them the Tricks

Improved study skills always lead to better grades. Memory tricks such as acronyms, word pictures, songs, and rhymes help children to retain information. Show your child how to study for tests by making and reviewing flash cards. Teach your child good test-taking techniques. For example, test grades improve when students look over the whole test and answer easy questions first. Teach your children to skip the more difficult questions and come back to them after answering the easy questions. Sometimes other questions on the test will give the student clues to the questions he skipped on the first pass.

Some children get "brain freeze" when taking tests. The solution to this is often as easy as taking practice tests at home. Our younger son, Blaize, who normally tests well, failed a number of "timed tests" in math before we discovered that he was having difficulty. In fact, he was at the very bottom of his class of twenty-seven students, even though he knew the answers. It was simply the pressure of having to beat the clock that unnerved him. We asked his teacher to give us some sample tests for practice at home and began giving Blaize several one-minute to five-minute timed tests each evening. After a few weeks, when timed tests were the norm rather than a novelty, he began to ace his tests. It took several months for him to rebound, and a lot of diligence on our part as parents, but now Blaize is at the top of his class in math.

School should be a fun and intellectually stimulating experience that prepares students for a lifetime of success. I encourage you to put these keys into practice to accelerate both your children's grades and their love of learning.

FREE BONUS #12
Special Report for Students—"The Top 20 Ways to Ace the Test and Improve Your Grades" ($29 value)

Yes, it is possible to get better grades *and* have more fun! This special report will show you how.

How to Motivate Teens and Young Adults

Now let's talk about how to motivate teens and young adults, starting with Phase Four of childhood, the dreaded teen years.

Parents often tell me how unmotivated their teenagers are. I generally challenge that assumption by saying, "The truth is that your teenagers are *extremely* motivated. They are motivated to do the things *they* want to do . . . watch TV, listen to music, surf the Net, text or talk on the phone to their friends, shop, and play video games!"

Therein lies the rub. How can you motivate teenagers to do what *you* want them to do? I respectfully submit that perhaps we are asking the wrong question. Our job as the parents, grandparents, and teachers of teenage children is not to make them do what they don't want to do—but to help them successfully navigate the teen years and equip them for adulthood.

Phase Four: Teenagers
(Ages 12–19)

Psychologist Dr. James Dobson uses the metaphor of a turbulent, alligator-infested river to describe the teen years. He says that our children ride this raging river in a little canoe. Our job as parents is to help them get downstream without being tossed overboard. Dr. Dobson wisely advises parents not to rock the boat on nonessential issues. Ignore the messy bedroom—close the door—and save the big guns for crucial confrontations about safety and morality.

YOUR QUESTION: How do I motivate my teenager to be responsible and communicate respectfully?

THE ANSWER: Strap yourself in. Now the real work begins.

A few months ago, I spoke at a national youth conference for several thousand teenagers. Afterward, a group of girls came to speak to me. One of them said, "We wanted to tell you that you have an ability to connect with our generation unlike anyone we've ever met before." I think that is the greatest compliment I've ever received in my life.

Communicating with teenagers is an art. Parents can unintentionally become "correction machines" that constantly dispense criticism, advice, demands, and disapproval. It's no wonder that teenagers clam up and become sullen in the face of such parental censure. The following tips are based on information from the excellent book by Adele Faber and Elaine Mazlish, *How to Talk So Teens Will Listen and Listen So Teens Will Talk*:

1. Listen without negative comment. Teens don't want you to fix all their problems. Just listen. Don't disagree with their thoughts or criticize their judgments. Listening makes them feel understood.

2. Speak to teenagers with courtesy and respect. Expressing your annoyance and exasperation does not facilitate good communication. Instead, it causes teens to respond with their own irritation and frustration.

3. Communicate using nonwords. When your teenager is talking, acknowledge their feelings with a sound. You can grunt or say, "Uh-huh," "Yeah," "Oh," "Mmm," "Uh," or "Wow" periodically to encourage them to continue. This takes a surprising amount of practice, but it really works.

4. Be brief. Long lectures teach teens to tune out. When you have a conflict with your teenager, it's better to put your objections, and the reasons for them, in writing. It dials down the emotion and kids respond better.

5. Instead of nagging, say it with a word. When your children leave the lights on, rather than complaining that you don't own the electric company, simply say, "Lights!" It's amazing how well kids respond to just a word. You'll get better results with less irritation.

Motivational DNA and Teens

In Chapter 1, I discussed the frustration I experienced for several years with my son Zack. I was in tears almost every day because of the conflicts we had. The problem, as it turned out, was not my son, but me. Zack (a classic PSE) is challenge-driven. In order to motivate him, I have to appreciate his forceful personality and work with it. I have to respect his budding leadership abilities and give him structured freedom.

Zack's primary motivational factor is Production. His greatest desire is control. A dominant child can be very difficult to live with. His or her undeveloped leadership potential can come across as bossy, demanding, and bratty. When I started to understand Zack's motivational type, I changed my parenting style and the results were phenomenal. Earlier you learned about the different motivational factors, which should help you identify your child's motivational type. Once you profile your children's Motivational DNA, you have a huge advantage in parenting them.

Let me also mention that while raising a forceful child is tricky, parenting a compliant child presents its own set of challenges. If you have a kind, affectionate, obedient child, it's easy to coast along as a parent, but we cannot let our compliant children raise themselves. We still need to encourage them to do their best. It is also important to give them the interaction and affirmation that they need to thrive. A potential problem for compliant children comes in the form of peer pressure. Because of their need to please, compliant kids may go along with the crowd rather than take a stand and defy the group. Compliant children need to be taught how to stand their ground and that it's okay to say no.

Kids are different, and the way that we interact with them cannot rely on a one-size-fits-all approach. Although you may love each of your children the same, you have to treat them differently. Our principles don't change, but our practices must. In other words, our core values should remain consistent, but we must adapt how we communicate with our children to get the best results.

How to Stay Connected to Your Kids

Communication is imperative for staying connected to your teens. Another way to stay connected is to attend their sports games and performances. It is impossible to overstate how important this is to teenagers. Even if they act embarrassed by the presence of their parents, your teenagers are secretly thrilled that you are there. Your attendance affirms that their interests are important to you and that you are proud of them. Your absence, however, creates distance and detachment.

My parents were missing in action. My father and mother were both hardworking businesspeople with many positive qualities, but they were absent when I was a teenager. They were not involved in my life, schooling, or friendships. I take responsibility for my actions, but sometimes I wonder if I would have taken drugs or dropped out of school if my parents had been more present. Consider me a cautionary tale. Good parents, at the very least, stay informed.

Get to know your teenagers' friends and their friends' families. Become acquainted with your children's teachers and with what your kids are learning at school. Monitor your teens' entertainment habits. What movies and TV shows are your kids watching? Where do they spend their time when they are online? What music are they listening to on their iPods?

A few years ago, Zack wanted to see a particular movie with his friends. I looked up an online review and decided not to let him see it. Of course, he was upset.

"But, Mom, why can't I go? Other parents are letting their kids go," he complained.

"There are several other movies you can see," I said. "But that movie is tasteless and full of sexual innuendo."

"You think if I go to the movie I'm going to have sex and turn into a delinquent?"

"No, I don't, Zack. That's not my point," I said. "Frankly, that movie is inappropriate at any age. It's just not a good movie. You might feel like walking out of a tasteless movie like that, but would you actually get up and go—even if it meant leaving your friends in the theater to watch the movie without you? In the future, I believe, you would. I'm just not sure you're at that level of maturity yet."

Zack went quiet. I had accidentally struck a nerve. I challenged him to step up to a new level of leadership, and he respected that.

RECOMMENDED RESOURCES

I use several movie-review Web sites, but my favorite is Plugged In (www.pluggedinonline.com). This site dissects movies, informing you of any violent content, sexual situations, profanity, and drug- and alcohol-related scenes in the films. It tells you both the positive and negative elements of the movies. Plugged In does not recommend films, but it gives parents enough information to assist them as they set standards for acceptable entertainment.

When teenagers start to drive, parents are justifiably worried. Young people have an average of three accidents between the ages of sixteen and twenty. The leading cause of death for teenagers is auto accidents, and teen drivers are four times more likely to lose their lives in accidents than are older, more experienced drivers. For these reasons, if you can afford it, I suggest getting a GPS tracking system for your new drivers. GPS tracking helps you to monitor your teen drivers. These systems allow you to find out by phone or computer where your teen driver is right now, or has been. You can also be notified by text message when drivers exceed your specified speed limit or when the vehicle is taken to an area that you have restricted.

The last resource I recommend is pen and paper. I have seen what a major impact cards, notes, and letters make to children. In Zack's case, the effects of the written word were substantial. Zack was an early bloomer. I thought teenage confrontations would begin at thirteen. With Zack, they began at ten.

I was stunned when, at age eleven, Zack told me he wanted to date. He argued relentlessly to be allowed to take a girl to the movies and out for a meal. At eleven! I said, "Son, everything you want will come to you, but not as fast as you want. You'll be allowed to date and to drive. You'll have freedom. You'll get an apartment and move out of our house. Everything you want will happen, but it is going to feel impossibly slow. I'm sorry. I wish I could speed it up for you, but I can't. It takes time to grow up and it takes responsibility to earn privileges."

The following two letters to Zack represent my most difficult and wonderful moments of motherhood. I extend special thanks to Zack, who allowed me to share these letters with you.

On Accepting Correction (At Age 12)

November 14, 2005
Dear Zack,

You've been so sweet with your words and actions for a long time now. You earned this letter! Thank you for making the effort to grow. We saw how hard you worked to break out of the shy trap and you did it! The way you have grown in confidence is just astounding. We are very impressed!

We know that growing up isn't easy. Being twelve can be stressful. We know it's not easy to accept correction in a mature way—most adults have never even learned that. But you work hard on your character and it shows. You have great character, a loving heart, and a generous spirit.

Our friends often comment on how well you conduct yourself. We are proud of how composed you are, and how you show respect to us and other adults. That will take you a long way in life. So many people have no clue how to carry themselves with dignity.

Once again you amaze us. You really do have an incredible capacity for change and growth. That is one of the greatest assets a person can have—and you've got it!

We love you, Zack, and are so proud of you!
Mom

On Maturity (At Age 13)

December 18, 2006

Incredible, Smart, Handsome, Wonderful Teenager,

    As you know by now, when I'm super happy with you, I write you a letter. Well, this is one that you TOTALLY deserve! You have amazed Dad and me with your outstanding attitude. You've definitely gone to a whole new level!

    Working hard at school, going out of your way to help around the house, using your position as big brother to encourage Blaize, and watching you make wise decisions . . . well, it's been beautiful to behold! Not only that—and I cannot possibly overstate this—I am thrilled to see that you were invited to be in advanced placement math. You thoroughly deserve that. You worked at improving your grades and your teachers noticed. You inspire me!

    Your openness, affection, and agreeability have been a joy to Dad and me. I'm also pleased to see your levelheadedness with girls. You have made an amazing shift from even just a year ago. You are a leader of the finest kind—one that brings out the best in others. Anyone can lead people in rebellion, but it takes a dynamic leader—a real man—to lead others in a positive direction.

    Zack, with all my heart, I am honored to call you my son.

    With love, admiration, and esteem,

    Mom

Phase Five: Young Adults (Ages 20–25)

As the parents of young adults, our job is to release them and let them fly. I assure you, although you are letting them go, your children still need you. Young adults want your friendship, your wisdom, occasional help, and accountability. Ironically, they want exactly what they were trying to escape from when they were teens!

YOUR QUESTION: What now?

THE ANSWER: Enjoy what you worked for. Admire the person your child has become.

I've had the privilege of mentoring hundreds of teens and young adults over the years. Many of them are like my own children, and it has been wonderful to see them grow into successful adults. During the Young Adult Phase, we transition into a new role as parents. Now is the time to let our kids make their own decisions.

Respect your child and treat him or her as a responsible adult. Offer advice only when asked. Your children may not have the same tastes or values that you have, but avoid criticizing their choices. Respect their privacy and their need to have independent lives. You can no longer baby-proof the world for your adult children. They have to stand on their own two feet. After a few wobbly steps, we usually discover that they can walk just fine.

Every child presents unique challenges, and so does each stage of their development. I wish I could tell you that there is a quick fix: "Just do this one thing and your kids will be motivated for life." Sorry, it doesn't work that way. Raising motivated children requires heavy lifting. If we want better children, we have to step up and be better parents.

FREE BONUS #13
Executive Book Summaries of Ten Personal Development Bestsellers to Help Your Teenage and Adult Children Succeed in Life. ($85 value)

I've selected summaries of ten of my favorite books for your teenage and adult children. These summaries will provide your kids with insights on how to build the skills and character they need to experience lasting success in life:

- *How Full Is Your Bucket?* by Tom Rath and Donald O. Clifton
- *Developing the Leader Within You* by John Maxwell
- *Failing Forward* by John Maxwell
- *Who Moved My Cheese?* by Spenser Johnson
- *Principle-Centered Leadership* by Stephen R. Covey
- *How to Win Friends and Influence People* by Dale Carnegie
- *The Power of Positive Living* by Norman Vincent Peale
- *Top Performance* by Zig Ziglar
- *The Traveler's Gift* by Andy Andrews
- *Destination Success* by Dwight Bain

PART FOUR

STRATEGIC GOAL ACHIEVEMENT

Start Strong

I'd like to ask you a question: *What do you really want out of life?* Think about it. I'm asking you this question because I want you to live the life of your dreams—and I know it's possible. When I started producing seminars, I was a young, uneducated, inexperienced, unemployed, and flat broke former drug addict. If there's a recipe for failure, I was the embodiment of it. Yet today, I say with all gratitude, I live the life of my dreams.

And I can tell you with certainty: It doesn't matter where you came from. Your past does not determine your future. It doesn't matter what you know or who you know. Everyone has the opportunity to improve their quality of life. But it starts with this question: What do you really, really, *really* want?

The purpose of this part of the book is to break down the essential skills of goal achievement. I am going to set you up for success. In order for me to do that, you need to be very clear about what *you* want. What do you wish to have in your life that you don't have now? Who would you like to be? What do you want to do with your life that you are not already doing? How would you like to contribute to society? What dreams totally light you up? What makes your heart smile just thinking about it? How do you want to be remembered? What would you like your legacy to be?

In Appendix B, I've included a place for you to list the top ten things you really want in life that you don't yet have. What do you really want? If you take the time to drill deep and answer that question for yourself, it will become a life compass for you. Knowing what you really want will create a benchmark that will guide you in goal achievement. It will save you from hopping down rabbit trails that have nothing to do with what you most desire. Take a break right now, turn to Appendix B, and identify the top ten things that you most passionately want out of life.

When I was nineteen years old, I made a list of lifetime goals for myself—they were ambitious, lofty dreams that even by my own estimation were somewhat crazy. It was a no-holds-barred, miracle-sized,

---

PRINCIPLE #1: BEGIN AT THE END
It Wasn't Raining When Noah
Built the Ark

You cannot control the future, but you can plan for it.
Create a clearly defined picture of what you really
want in life. This picture should be so vivid that seeing it
in your imagination energizes you *right now*.
Visualize the end at the beginning.

gargantuan life wish list. My list included things like traveling around the world, becoming fluent in a foreign language, learning a musical instrument, marrying my soul mate, and having children—as well as spiritual, health, career, and financial goals.

Do you want to know the most shocking thing about that list? I thought it would take several lifetimes to accomplish everything on my list. But I achieved all forty of the goals I put down on that list before I turned forty! At the age of forty, I made another list of goals for the second half of my life. Buoyed by success the first time around, my new goals are even more audacious.

I am convinced that God loves dreamers (and doers) with big dreams. There is an element of both faith and hope in every dream. Yet there is a chasm of difference between *dreams* and *goals*. Anyone can dream dreams. But when you create a goal, write it down, and actively initiate and implement the steps necessary to get to that goal, the process of achievement has begun.

From the time that I made my first list of goals at the age of nineteen to this day, the very process of writing down my goals has proven to have a profound impact on my life. It has shaped the destiny and direction of my life.

In this chapter, I am going to use my story as a backdrop for identifying the principles that you need to start strong. These principles relate to all goals—whether your goal is to start a business, double your income, get in shape, or organize a department. In every case, the same strategies will apply. As I take you on my journey, think about your own. Extrapolate lessons that you can apply to your own life.

Starting America's Biggest Business Seminars

I met my husband, Peter, at a writers' conference on the campus of Wheaton College in Illinois. I was a recent college grad—in fact, I was celebrating my graduation by attending the writers' workshop. Both Peter and I were already involved in event planning. He was a young entrepreneur who owned a sales training company. I was a motivational speaker who was facilitating and speaking at youth events.

Peter and I connected instantly. He had a certain spark—and it wasn't just his red hair. He was smart, engaging, and funny. Although I wasn't romantically interested in Peter, I enjoyed his company. We hung out in Chicago that weekend, seeing the sights, checking out local restaurants, and talking nonstop. Before the weekend had ended, Peter had begun to set up a business seminar in Florida, where I lived at the time, so that he would have an excuse to see me again. A few weeks later, Peter called and said, "I'm doing a seminar in your city and if you'd like tickets, let me know. I'd love it if you could attend."

When Peter came to Florida for the seminar, I had the opportunity to introduce him to my family and friends. My parents immediately loved Peter. After knowing him for all of twenty minutes, my mother pulled me aside and whispered, "I want you to know that if you are ever interested in marrying this man, you have my blessing." I laughed and said, "Peter and I are just friends, Mom."

Six months later, Peter and I were on a riverboat, cruising down the Mississippi River in New Orleans, exchanging vows. What can I say? Friendship turned to love.

After a six-week honeymoon in Thailand, Singapore, Hong Kong, and Malaysia, Peter and I made a brief stop in Canada to visit Peter's parents. Then we flew home to New Orleans and settled into our newlywed apartment. We began our marriage with a blank canvas. We had decided to work through our plans over breakfast one morning. We sat down at the kitchen table with legal pads and pens. It was so long ago, laptop computers had not even been invented yet!

"Okay," Peter said, taking the lead, "let's create a life that will reflect our passions. What's the first thing that comes to mind when you think about what you'd like our life together to look like?"

"I want us to work together. I don't want to go our separate ways every morning and reconnect over dinner each night. I want us to really live life together."

We each jotted down on our legal pads: 1. *Work together.*

"What kind of work would you like to do?" Peter asked.

"I don't think we need to completely reconstruct this. We're both good at public speaking. We enjoy promoting and producing events. Are you still interested in doing that?"

"Absolutely," Peter said. "I don't know of any other forum that gives us the opportunity to interact with people one-on-one in the same way that seminars do. I'm committed to making a positive impact on others. I agree with you. We should be doing public events."

We scribbled on our notepads: 2. *Public events.*

"All right," I said. "What resources do we have financially?"

We both began laughing at that question. In a moment of infatuated impetuousness, we had decided to drain all our savings to pay for our wedding, honeymoon, and three months of living expenses. The clock was ticking. We had six weeks of oxygen left before the bill collectors started knocking.

"Okay, so we don't have financial resources," I said. "But we have other resources that we can use to make money. Let's list those."

PRINCIPLE #2: TAKE INVENTORY
You Already Have Most of
What You Need

List all of the personal resources that you can use to achieve your goal. Include natural talents, developed skills, financial resources, and organizational tools that will help you attain your goal.

**PRINCIPLE #3: DON'T INVENT
IF YOU CAN REINVENT
The Early Bird May Get the Worm, but the
Second Mouse Gets the Cheese**

It takes more effort and energy to create than to re-create.
Identify a successful individual or organization and
model what they are doing. If you do exactly what they do,
you should get similar results. But if you do it better,
faster, smarter, and more cost-effectively,
you will get *better* results.

Peter began. "I'm good with numbers," he said.

This was actually an incredible understatement. Peter is a mathematical genius. In the ninth grade he placed first in the national math contest for all of Canada. Peter's ability with numbers is astonishing.

"You're great with numbers and I'm good with words," I said. "That's a powerful combination!"

"We both enjoy sales and marketing," Peter continued.

"And you have a lot of experience with logistics and advertising," I added. "We also have time. We don't have children or other obligations. We can focus our energy on our business without interruption or other distractions. We can work at any time of the day or night. And we can do it together, so it will be fun."

"You're gorgeous!" Peter said, smiling.

"Back at ya, baby! But we're veering off topic! Come on, we're on a roll here. What other resources do we have?"

"We know how to create a compelling event at a good price that makes people want to attend."

"That's true," I said. "But we don't know how to gather a large

---

**PRINCIPLE #4: IDENTIFY YOUR
CONSTRAINTS
If You Are Willing to Admit
Your Faults, You Have One Less
Fault to Admit**

List every obstacle that you are likely to encounter and
every challenge that you will need to overcome in order to
achieve your goal. Next, come up with at least three ways
to overcome each of those obstacles.

---

crowd. Right now our audiences are fifty to one hundred people. That's good enough to make a living, but it's not enough to make a life. I want to have a greater impact than reaching just a few thousand people each year."

"Agreed," Peter said. "We'll work on that. So let's go down that trail for a bit. What obstacles are we going to encounter putting on big events?"

"Money," I said, stating the obvious. "We're going to need financing to do large events. How are we going to overcome that challenge?"

"Right now people pay to attend our events when they arrive and register at the door. Suppose we were to sell tickets to our seminar in advance and then use the money to fund the promotion and execution of the event? What do you think of that?"

"I think we ought to test it. It's a model that has the potential of growing our business without requiring a large initial capital investment. It's a little risky, but if we prepay for the venue we eliminate the danger of not being able to execute a seminar that people have already bought tickets for."

"Good. Other obstacles?"

"Well, we're young," I said. "I don't consider that a limitation. We have the energy and enthusiasm of youth, but I've found that older people can be apprehensive about entrepreneurs in their twenties."

"True. Let's put youth on both lists," Peter said. "It's a resource that we can utilize, but it can also be a handicap, so let's put it on the obstacles list too. I'd also add inexperience to the obstacles list. We have experience in seminar promotion, but we don't know what hurdles we'll have to leap to get to the next level and do it on a large scale."

"Okay, I think we should talk about how to overcome the obstacles that we're going to face," I said. "But first let's write down some of the people or organizations who may be able to help us. We're not limited to our own resources. Perhaps we can utilize the time, brainpower, and talent of others."

"We should add another speaker to our seminars," Peter said. "If we partner with someone who is well known and already has an established fan base, we can market to their core audience and sell tickets to them. We could send brochures out to their mailing lists and potentially double or triple the size of our audience."

"That's a great plan," I said. "Any ideas about who we should invite to speak with us?"

"I know this sounds crazy," Peter said, "but the first name that comes to mind is Ronald Reagan."

"*President* Ronald Reagan?"

PRINCIPLE #5: CREATE ALLIANCES
It's Not Whom You Know,
but What They Know

Enlist the people and organizations that can assist you.

"Yeah, that's the guy!"

"You're right. That sounds crazy. What else have you got?"

"Nothing right now, but I want to take some time to pray about it."

"For sure! You should definitely pray about it! Are there any other people or organizations that you think would be able to help us?" I asked.

"Nothing really comes to mind. What about you?"

"I know an amazing woman who would be an awesome fit with us. Her name is Joan. She's smart, attractive, and has a flair for public relations. I think she could do anything we asked her to do . . . accounting, ticket sales, operations, you name it."

"Great! Let's check with her and see if she's available. I think we should start planning our first seminar right away."

"How exciting!" I said.

A few days later, Peter came out of his office with a curious expression on his face. I knew that he had been praying about whom we should invite to speak with us, but I didn't know that he'd spent *four solid hours* petitioning the Almighty. Peter has always had a capacity for prayer that awes me. I am a spiritual slug in comparison.

"So? What did you get?" I asked.

"Two names," Peter said. "Zig Ziglar and Ronald Reagan."

"Wow! Okay. Well, maybe we should start with Zig."

In 1987, Zig Ziglar was a famous author and motivator who was doing small seminars around the country. He had an established network of seminar promoters that he worked with exclusively. Each of his promoters had a specified geographic territory that spanned the country from coast to coast. When we contacted Zig's office to invite him to speak for us, they politely declined. But we persisted.

"What do we need to do?" we asked. "What if we prepay Zig's speaker fee? What if we guarantee a big audience?"

Zig's office asked us to submit financial documents and a business

PRINCIPLE #6: PLAN FOR
INCREMENTAL SUCCESS
Never Test the Depth of a River
with Both Feet

**Think big, but start small. Look for reproducible strategies.
Even if you hit a home run once, you won't win the game
unless you can do it again and again and again.
Don't make the amateur mistake of
overleveraging yourself.**

plan, which we did. We also volunteered to do the seminar in any city that they chose. After many weeks of negotiation, we were allowed to produce a seminar in New Orleans, where we lived at the time, because no other promoter wanted to go there. New Orleans was known in the industry as "the promoter's graveyard." Everyone who staged a seminar in New Orleans lost their shirt. On that encouraging note, we began to ramp up for our first seminar as a married couple.

We did it all. We booked the grand ballroom at a local hotel. We designed and printed the brochures. Peter made sales calls, business to business, to sell tickets. I did telemarketing and bookkeeping, and fulfilled ticket orders from our kitchen table. New Orleans had indeed earned its poor reputation in the seminar business. It was a grueling few months. It was tough to motivate business owners to send their employees to our event. We thought that having Zig Ziglar on our program would make the process easy, because Zig was a wonderful speaker. But marketing, not speakers, is the real key to the event business, and we learned that the hard way.

After several months of exhausting effort, we held the seminar. I

PRINCIPLE #7: COUNT THE COST
Incoming Fire Has the Right of Way

Brace yourself for unexpected adversity.
Attaining your goal is going to cost you—count on it.
Decide in advance if you are willing and able to
pay the price. Do you have what it takes to hold on
financially and emotionally?

have never been so tired in my life. Peter and I were working eighteen-hour days. We weren't eating or sleeping properly, but the labor paid off. We had a huge crowd of several thousand people at the event, which was terrific for any city, even a major market like Chicago or Dallas. But in New Orleans, the promoter's graveyard, it was nothing short of astonishing.

After the seminar, as I collapsed into bed, relishing the idea of getting a full night's sleep, my husband burst into the room. "Guess what?" Peter said, "Zig and his CEO want to meet with us tomorrow morning before they fly out."

"Are you serious? What time?" I asked. "Please tell me they have an afternoon flight!"

"They want to meet for breakfast at six A.M."

"You must be joking! You're going to have to pry me out of bed. I've been looking forward to a good sleep for months!"

"What do you suppose they want to talk about?" Peter asked.

"It's my guess that they are interested in doing more seminars with us. We managed to execute a successful seminar with an attendance that tops what they see in most big cities. And we did it on our first attempt—in a city that none of their other promoters even wanted to come to. From their perspective, that probably merits further discussion with us. What do you think?"

"I think you're probably right," Peter said. "We'd better get some sleep. . . . We've got an early start!"

Blurry-eyed and sleep-deprived, we arrived at breakfast the next morning. Sure enough, Zig wanted to discuss the possibility of working with us more in the future.

We met with Zig and his team several more times over the ensuing months. They decided to let us promote events in small cities where their other promoters were not producing seminars. So we went from city to city, and as we grew in experience, our crowds grew as well. It soon became evident that Zig's largest seminars were being produced by his youngest promoters.

As for Peter and me, we were having the time of our lives. It was fulfilling to know that we were making a positive difference in the lives of so many people. We had the wonderful experience of being able to call on businesses and work at the grassroots level to market the events. Then we'd celebrate by hosting a dynamic, high energy seminar. After that, we'd move on to the next city, meet new people, make new friends, and explore new places.

Before long we did indeed become Zig's exclusive promoters, and we've had the joy of serving him for more than two decades. Over the years our seminars outgrew hotel ballrooms. Then they outgrew convention centers. Today we host events in America's largest sports arenas. But one thing has remained the same—we have always invited Zig to be a part of our seminars, from that day until now.

And whatever happened with Ronald Reagan? Well, that's another story! It's one for the next chapter.

FREE BONUS #14

From Tamara's Personal Archive of Celebrity Interviews—
"How to Be a Visionary Leader" by President Gerald Ford.
The former United States president discusses the six
fundamentals of leadership. (Priceless value)

Before ascending to the office of president, Gerald Ford served as Vice President, and before that he served twenty-five years in the House of Representatives—eight as Republican Minority Leader. Although he was unassuming and even self-deprecating, few people share his legacy and longevity of leadership. This exclusive article will give you President Ford's secrets to enduring leadership.

Sustain the Action

I n 1989, I wrote a letter to President Ronald Reagan, inviting him to speak at one of our seminars. At the time, I was twenty-five years old and a complete unknown.

Curiously, President Reagan didn't write me back.

I wrote him another letter.

He didn't respond.

I sent another invitation.

Nothing.

I was beginning to think the President was ignoring me.

I wrote him again.

His secretary wrote back saying President Reagan regretfully declined the offer to speak at one of our seminars.

I ignored the secretary.

I wrote another letter.

And another.

And another.

My husband and I began to phone the President's office regularly.

I'd call and say, "Hi, this is Tamara Lowe. Has President Reagan decided to speak for us yet?"

The secretary would say, "Hi, Tamara. The answer is the same as last week. The President is not going to speak for you."

My husband would call back the following week and say, "Hi, this is Peter Lowe."

The secretary would say, "Hi, Peter. The President is not going to speak for you."

It finally came down to a weekly two-word dialogue: We'd say, "Hi," she'd say, "No!" We'd all laugh, and I'd call back the next week.

This went on for four years!

President Reagan eventually concluded that while we were undeniably thickheaded, we weren't stalkers or a threat to national security . . . and we weren't going to go away. He finally decided to speak for us. The Great Communicator did his first seminar with us in Phoenix, Arizona. Of course, the event was a standing-room-only, sellout success.

The Devil of Discouragement

In the pursuit of any significant goal, you will get discouraged. You will feel like giving up. Guaranteed. Every major endeavor comes with a special bonus: the opportunity to fail publicly. In order to succeed, you have to be prepared to wrestle with fear, wrangle with doubts, and slap down the temptation to quit. In short, you have to sustain your motivation and power past the fear of failure.

Soon after we did our first seminar with President Reagan, our business grew—and so did our family. We were now the proud parents of a beautiful baby boy. I had not been eager to start a family while we were building our company and dealing with the challenges of growth, management, and cash flow. I kept telling Peter, "It's not a good time for me to get pregnant. Let's wait until after our Dallas event."

Dallas would come and go, but by that time a new challenge would emerge. I'd say, "Honey, it's not a good time to start a family. I need to launch our telemarketing department, and that's going to be too much to deal with while I'm pregnant." Once the telecenter was up and running smoothly, another crisis demanded my attention.

Finally, Peter said, "There will never be a perfect time to have a baby, Tamara. We just need to do it anyway." He was right. One morning I was reading my Bible and came across this verse in Ecclesiastes 11:4:

If you wait for perfect conditions, you will never get anything done.

So, despite my hesitation, trepidation, and imperfect timing, we decided to plunge into parenthood. As all new parents will testify, having a baby produces wonderful joy and terrible stress. I was a mess of conflicting emotions. Zack was a breathtakingly gorgeous child. I could not pry my eyes off of him. I had the complete opposite of postpartum depression. I was blissed out of my mind. On the other hand, business had been my life and the demands of motherhood threw me out of my orbit. I felt isolated and overwhelmed by being sequestered with a squalling, albeit beautiful, bundle of neediness.

The arrival of our firstborn marked the beginning of a very difficult season for us. Our business had grown exponentially, but we didn't have the management infrastructure to keep up with the growth. For the first time, I did not know the names of all our staff members, and that plagued me. I had photos taken of everyone and committed myself to memorizing the names, faces, and job titles of more than 300 full-time employees and part-time contractors.

Our seminar schedule was also exploding. In 1993, we did fifty massive, large-venue seminars and it nearly did us in. The media attention that we received was a full-time job in and of itself. We were featured in *Time* and *People* magazines. The television news shows *60 Minutes, Dateline,* and *20/20* all sent camera crews to cover our events. In every city, we were interviewed by reporters from the local newspapers as well as all of the television news affiliates. I toted baby Zack around the country, ran our business, emceed seminars, mingled with speakers, entertained the press, and managed events, all with an infant on my hip.

At the same time this was going on, I was also doing corporate speaking engagements all over the world. By the time Zack was three years old, he had traveled with me to more than thirty countries. It was a whirlwind time of great highs mixed with enormous, crushing pressure. I can't tell you the number of times I wanted to cash in our chips and call it a day. When you are tempted to quit, remember that the weight of difficulty is the acid test of leadership. Losers crumble under the load, but leaders buck up.

All right, let's take a break and draw a lesson from what I've shared so far. After the initial blast that propels you when you start in on a goal, there will be a slow leak of motivation. I don't want to discourage you by saying this, but it is the biting reality. The demands of life will vie for your attention. Perhaps you'll make some good progress at the beginning, but then be lulled into a state of contentment and start to coast. Before long the gentle cruise may come to a standstill, and if you're not careful, you can quickly lose the progress that you already made. This is why sustained motivation is so important. This is why the skills you acquired using Motivational DNA are absolutely imperative.

How can you sustain motivation? I'll say it again: You must appeal to your motivational patterns. Producers, push yourselves to get results. Connectors, surround yourselves with a support network to assist you. Stabilizers, stick to the plan! Variables, if you're bored, shake things up! Internals, focus on the outcome. Externals, take advantage of opportunities. Are you feeling discouraged? Do you feel like quitting? Now is the time to use the principles of Motivational DNA to create positive momentum.

Cooperate with Your Motivational Design

Let me give you an example of how I used Motivational DNA to sustain motivation and achieve a challenging goal. For decades I struggled to exercise regularly. The amount of travel that I do makes sticking with a consistent fitness program next to impossible. In the past, I'd begin a new sport, aerobics class, or gym membership with great excitement . . . then my enthusiasm would rapidly evaporate. Within a few weeks, my good intentions morphed into a bag of Doritos and whatever cardiovascular benefits can be gained from watching a heart-pounding episode of *24*.

I condemned myself for my inconsistency, giving myself mental "pep talks" that went something like this:

What's wrong with you? You've got to stick to an exercise program! Who cares what you want to do? Just make yourself do it! If you don't exercise, you're going to pay the price for it as you age. You want to be around to see your children and future grandchildren grow up, don't you? Well, lace up those running shoes, Grandma, and get out the door!

My pep talk did absolutely nothing to motivate me. If anything, it depressed me. I was stuck in a cycle of starts and stops that did not move me toward my goal.

I didn't recognize it at the time, but my exercise goals had been driven by a strategy that would be highly effective for a Stabilizer. However, for a Variable like myself, it was incredibly de-motivating. Do you remember the basic tenet of Motivational DNA? *What motivates one person can de-motivate another.* I was demanding inflexible structure and rigid consistency from myself when I'm not designed for that type of motivation. Once I understood that my dominant motivational factor is Variety, I intentionally took a new approach. I reconfigured my exercise plan, and I'm delighted to tell you that for the past several years I have consistently worked out five days a week, whether I am in America or Zaire, Australia or Zimbabwe.

Here's how I did it: I began with a ridiculously easy goal. I needed a challenge so small that it would be impossible for me to fail. I asked, "What is the bare minimum that I need to do in order to be fit?" When taking on a tough goal, it is important to clarify our outcomes. We need to know exactly what we are shooting for so the target is clear and easy to hit.

I learned that most adults require only twenty minutes of vigorous exercise a day, five days a week, to get in great shape. That sounded simple enough, so I tried it. On days when I was tired or busy I did just twenty minutes, but most of the time twenty minutes became thirty to ninety minutes without much effort. I did some sort of cardio exercise every weekday, plus weight lifting two to four times a week.

My twenty-minute plan, however, was not the complete solution. I needed more than a new program to keep me on track for the long haul. I needed to know *what to do when my motivation started to fade.* The real key to my success was the transformational power unlocked by Motivational DNA. As a Variable, I simply cannot force myself to do the same thing day after day and find it satisfying. My health was being sabotaged by monotony. Every new exercise program that I tried was enjoyable for a short period of time and then I'd tire of it. This is typical for Variables.

I required a strategy that would appeal to my unique motivators—one that factored in my travel-related challenges and unpredictable schedule. I needed a boredom-proof plan for busy people. Here's the solution I hit upon: Every day I pick some sort of cardio activity that I do for a minimum of twenty minutes. I select my activity—and the amount of time that I exercise—based on my mood. What do I feel like doing today? How much time do I have to spare? How much energy do I have? Is the weather nice enough to allow me to exercise outdoors? My exercise routine is now flexible enough to be determined by these questions. A capricious method, I admit, dictated solely by my whim at the moment—and it totally works for me.

Some days I take a run on the beach or swim. Other days I walk with Nordic poles, which is a phenomenal workout, by the way. I spend part of the winter in Colorado, where I snowshoe or snowboard almost every day. For some reason, I never get tired of winter sports. If the weather is bad, I go to the gym and hop on whichever cardio machine appeals to me the most. I also invested in a folding bicycle. Many days, on my way home from the office, I pull over at a park or scenic stretch of sidewalk, unfold my bike, and pedal away. This allows me to work exercise into my day and still meet my Variety need to explore and discover. Plus, I never get bored anymore.

When I lift weights, I do it at the beginning and the end of the week. I don't pick a specific day to strength-train, as long as I do it at least twice a week. This kind of freedom liberates me. I don't feel constrained by a demanding, etched-in-stone routine. I have options. And it's travel-friendly. Most important, I achieve my goal of daily exercise and I'm in better shape now than I was in my twenties.

Recently, I took a VO_2 max test, which measures aerobic capacity, heart and pulmonary functions, and the amount of oxygen your body is able to use during exercise. It is a grueling test that normally costs thousands of dollars and is primarily used for elite athletes. I was wired up to an EKG and fitted with a head harness. A clothespin was clipped to my nose and a plastic tube was put in my mouth to capture my every breath. Then I hopped onto a stationary bike and pushed myself to absolute exhaustion. When the results were calculated, the doctors were astonished and I was too. I scored 100 percent for my age.

As simple as it sounds, this one discovery—to cooperate with my motivational design rather than fighting against it—totally transformed my health. I went from being out of shape and constantly frustrated with my inability to stick to an exercise program to being a fit, energetic amateur athlete. I don't believe for a moment that I have some extraordinary achievement drive. My success is the result of the amazing technology of Motivational DNA.

Even in the writing of this book, I found that I had to cooperate with my unique motivational makeup in order to get the best results. Had I tried to write my book from beginning to end—from page 1 to page 267—it would have been excruciating. I wrote this book in five months, but if I had forced myself to write sequentially, from start to finish, it would have taken me well over a year. At the beginning of the process, I realized that I had two choices: I could stare at a glaring, blank computer screen and watch my cursor blink on and off—or I could follow my bliss. I gave myself permission to be erratic. I'd work on Chapter 2 for ten minutes and then jump to Chapter 11 for a bit. Today, I feel like writing Chapter 13. That's how a Variable operates.

Motivational DNA has completely transformed my thinking—not only in relation to my personal goals but also in the way that I interact with others. Now I understand how to motivate my children, friends, family, and employees. I appeal to their individual motivators and the results are fantastic.

Back to You

Perhaps you are in the midst of tackling a tough goal and you're starting to get weary. Remember, this is normal. You are not weak-willed. You're human. Let me take you back to Chapter 3 for a moment. Review the section at the end of the chapter headed "Now It's Your Turn." This time, please do the written exercises I recommend. How do I know that you didn't do it the first time? You're human. (Except for you Stabilizers—you're superhuman, and I know your forms are already filled out in exacting detail!)

To sustain motivation, you must cooperate with your motivational patterns. If you work the system, the system will work for you. Be patient. Life is not a sprint. It's an endurance sport. Big goals take time. There will be huge, looming obstacles to overcome. Sometimes life is unfair and bad things do happen to good people. But if you're feeling a little disheartened today, I have good news for you: The past is past. It's over and done. Yesterday does not determine your tomorrow. What you do today determines your future. Stick with the system. Don't worry about setbacks. Failure is not final unless you quit.

Michael Jordan said, "I've missed more than 9,000 shots in my career. I've lost almost 300 games. Twenty-six times, I've been trusted to take the game-winning shot and missed. I've failed over and over and over again in my life. And that is why I succeed."

Isn't that the truth? Jordan makes great points off the court too. Success and failure are Siamese twins. You can't have one without the other. I've made so many mistakes in business, it's a miracle that I'm still standing. I've hired the wrong people, I've made terrible decisions, and I've lost millions of dollars in a single day. But, if nothing else, I have done one thing right: I kept going.

When I wanted to fire everyone, including myself, I kept going.

While the naysayers and doomsdayers prophesied my demise, I kept going. When my dream was so dim it was barely a flicker, I stuck with it. In those early days, countless times I thought, *I'm nuts. President Reagan is never going to speak for me.* No President has ever rejected a woman more than Ronald Reagan rejected me! I got countless no's, but all I needed was one yes. So I kept writing letters and continued to phone his dear, long-suffering secretary. I kept at it for four years . . . and then, one day, the Gipper said yes.

FREE BONUS #15
Exclusive Special Report—"25 Money Strategies to Help You Succeed in Every Economy." ($49 value)

The only thing certain in today's economy is uncertainty. But there are things you can do to make sure you survive and thrive—regardless of the doom and gloom in the headlines. It all starts with strategy, and these 25 money strategies will help you weather *any* economic storm and come out on top!

Finish First

I woke up at dawn, stumbled into the kitchen, and brewed myself a cappuccino. Then I sat down at my kitchen table to read the *Wall Street Journal*. I could not believe my eyes. Had I not seen it in print, I never would have believed it.

There, on the front page of the *Wall Street Journal*, dressed head-to-toe like General George C. Patton, disgracing the American flag he had the gall to stand in front of, hand raised while waving a pearl-handled pistol over his little pinhead, was one of my business competitors.

The Patton impostor had rallied his entire organization to announce to the press that he was going to put my husband and me out of business. It wasn't even 6 A.M. and I was officially under siege. The headline, in bold newspaper print, proclaimed: **"THIS IS WAR!"** It was a direct quote from my costume-clad nemesis. *Well, good morning to you too, General Patton. Do the doctors know you've stopped taking your meds?*

The article went on to describe how the General had created a star-studded motivational seminar designed to crush us. He whipped his sales force into a frenzy and dispatched the combat-ready troops to Atlanta to sell tickets.

My competitor apparently had a penchant for dress-up. To advertise his seminar, he painted himself gold, donned a sandwich board, and stood on a street corner. That was his business plan. You can't make this stuff up, folks.

In the end, the theatrics—while admittedly amusing—were not enough. The *Wall Street Journal* reported that he lost $700,000 and had 23,000 fewer attendees than the seminar our company had produced at the Georgia Dome the previous year.

Gaining the Competitive Advantage

General Patton was not the first competitor to cross my path, but I have to give him credit, because he was certainly the most creative. The seminar business is a revolving door. I've seen hundreds of people get into it and hundreds of people get right back out. It is a high-risk, high-stress, low-margin business. It's possible to lose money faster than a five-year-old can slurp up a spaghetti noodle.

In business and in life, competition is a bittersweet reality. Unfortunately, hard work and a dream are not enough for anyone to become a standout success. To get ahead of the pack and finish first in your career, you need an arsenal of high-powered resources, or what I call "weapons of mass instruction." And none is more important than Motivational DNA.

So how can you outpace, outshine, outmaneuver, and outlast your competition? Lean in close, because I'm about to tell you a secret. This is the key to becoming number one in any field. No matter what your business, profession, or service, this is your ticket to the top. It's the magic bullet. It's how our team built the biggest seminar company in the world and have stayed at the apex of our industry for more than twenty-five years.

Here it is: *The secret to being number one . . . is being number one.*

I know; it's profound. Let me say it another way: *The real key to being the best . . . is being the best.* You must motivate yourself to learn more, do more, and be more than everyone else around you. You've got to work longer, smarter, and faster. You have to deliver the best product at the best price and have unsurpassed service to boot. You need to be knowledgeable, articulate, energetic, confident, competent, and courageous. *You have to be the best.*

Good enough is not good enough to succeed at the highest levels. Whether you are vying for market share, competing in an athletic event, or trying to win a promotion at work, finishing first requires breathtaking excellence. And that is where Motivational DNA comes in. Whether you are a Producer or a Connector, whether your primary need is Stability or Variety, you've got to be the best if you want to enjoy all of the Internal and External Awards of success.

I'll be the first to admit that you'll have to make some sacrifices to capture the top spot. But if you want to finish first, you have to pay the price. That means investing the time, effort, and money that it takes to develop superior skill. And once you've achieved your goal, once you are at the top of your profession or field, you have to *keep growing*. You must continue to build your skills. The finish line is always moving in life, so you constantly have to improve your product, your service, and yourself. If you don't, I guarantee that someone else will swoop in from behind and pass you by.

I Believe There Are Five High-Priority Areas In Our Lives:

- Career
- Finances
- Sense of spiritual fulfillment or purpose
- Relationships
- Health

In this last chapter, I'm going to spend a little time showing you how to use Motivational DNA to finish first in all five of these areas. This kind of balanced approach to life requires effort. Nailing four out of five, in my opinion, is not enough. If your business is thriving and you're making money hand over fist—but your teenager is on drugs and your marriage is disintegrating—you've failed. Likewise, if you are healthy and have fulfilling relationships—but your career is tanking and your bank account is anorexic—you are certainly not winning at life. "That's harsh," you might say. No, friend, it's the truth. As we honestly evaluate our lives, we sometimes need to face the brutal facts, no matter how painful they might be. The good news is that you can make adjustments to create balance in your life. And you can begin today. You really can have it all—but it calls for diligence and commitment. You have to be *motivated*.

Other motivational books will tell you that achieving success is simple and painless. Don't buy it. If it were easy, everyone would be happy, healthy, rich, making a positive difference in the world, involved in satisfying relationships, and living a spiritually fulfilling life. Please permit me to cut through the sugar-coated platitudes that masquerade as motivation and give you what you really need to succeed. I'm not going to mince words or worry about offending you. I might not tell you what you *want* to hear, but I will tell you what you *need* to hear. I respect your intelligence, so I'm going to give it to you straight. Strap yourself in; here are my motivational rules of life. Follow them and success will follow you.

Seven Career Builders
(and One Gigantic Career Killer)

1. Be Enthusiastic About Every Task—Especially the Unpleasant Ones!

This quality alone will distinguish you from 99.9 percent of people in the workplace. It will guarantee your promotion. It will ensure your elevation, secure your job, and accelerate your advancement. It will flat-out make you more money. When given an assignment, say, "YES! I would love to do that! I'll get right on it!" This is where motivation is crucial. You have to be enthusiastic about your job and yourself. You must be convinced that your efforts make a difference and that even undesirable duties merit your high-level performance.

Cultivate the attitude of a superachiever. How? Every single day, be cheerful, upbeat, and positive. Determine to be a ray of sunshine everywhere you go. Now that you know what your Drives, Needs, and Awards are, look for ways to engage them, even when doing unpleasant tasks.

2. When You Open Your Mouth—Say Something Worthwhile!

Learn to communicate skillfully. A rich, powerful vocabulary gives you the extra edge you need to express your ideas effectively, communicate with greater precision, and demonstrate your intellectual acumen.

At work, be friendly to people, but don't be chatty. Keep your conversations brief and to the point. Do not succumb to protracted social conversations on company time. It's irresponsible and wasteful. Rather than getting great results, you'll simply be wasting one of the most precious resources you have—your time.

Your written communications must also be exceptional. Avoid dashing off sloppy e-mails when you are pressed for time. Your writing should be clear, incisive, and free from spelling, punctuation, and grammatical errors. Well-composed correspondence is an attribute of excellence. Take that extra moment to spell-check everything you send out, including e-mails. Practice writing persuasively and passionately, so that your reader will be inspired to implement your recommendations.

3. Remember, the Customer Wears the Crown

It is imperative to connect with and cater to your customers. Do what you say you are going to do, *when* you say you are going to do it. Deliver on your promises. If it takes more time than you anticipated, so be it—work late to finish the job. And when a customer complains about one of your employees, do yourself a favor—agree with the customer. You can always listen to your employee's point of view later. First, agree with your customer and work to find a way to make him or her happy.

4. Be Punctual

Be on time all of the time. Better yet, be early.

5. Pay Attention to Your Appearance

Some jobs are inherently messy. But, generally, you should look good and be well-groomed, at work and in every professional capacity. Your hair should be styled, your nails clean and trimmed, your clothes pressed, your shoes shined, and your breath fresh. Your self-esteem, and the confidence you have in working with others, will skyrocket if you take a few simple steps to present your best self.

If you have problem skin, go to a dermatologist and get treatment for it. If you need to have your teeth fixed, make an appointment with your dentist and get it done. You don't want to hide your enthusiasm or smile because you are concerned about your teeth. Believe me, the time and money you spend to improve your appearance will come back to you many times over in better jobs, raises, bonuses, and self-confidence.

6. Be Organized

Don't let papers accumulate on your desk. Be efficient. A mile of piles in your office does not make you look busy; it makes you look disorganized, messy, frazzled, and overwhelmed. Learn now how to use the shortcut features on your computer. File everything. Invest the time needed to get organized. Then stay organized.

7. Focus on Your Strengths

As a speaker, I recognize that I don't have a booming voice like Zig Ziglar. Nor do I have the commanding stage presence of 6′2″ actor Samuel L. Jackson. What my audiences tell me I do have is charisma, humor, and the ability to inspire people to peak performance. The two most common comments I hear following my speeches are "You are so genuine" and "You are so funny." Those are my strengths. That is what impacts my audience. So I focus on those strengths. I became a student of stand-up comedy in order to master the elements of timing, delivery, and wordplay. And I work hard to make myself as transparent and authentic as I can be.

Do more of what you are good at. Be more of who you really are. If you have a natural aptitude for something, allow yourself to develop that gift. It will make you more successful. No matter what your Motivational DNA type, focusing on your strengths will make you better at what you do.

8. Be as Frugal with Your Company's Money as You Are with Your Own

Treat your organization's money as if it were your own. Ultimately, it is. If you gain the reputation for being fiscally prudent, you will advance in your career and end up making more money. Purchase only what is needed for success. Do not spend one cent of the company's money wastefully. Come in under budget. Don't inflate budget projections. Learn to get more done with less money, without undermining the customer. Never let cost cutting cause you to produce an inferior product or provide second-rate service—that is a gigantic career killer. It will not improve your business, but ultimately it will harm it.

Six Keys to Finishing Rich

One of the important ways that you can use your knowledge of Motivational DNA is to ensure that you are making wise financial decisions. Taking care of yourself and your family with a solid financial strategy safeguards and improves your standard of living—and actually enhances your motivation in other areas as well.

9. Work to Develop Multiple Streams of Income

A number of financial advisors recommend this, and I wholeheartedly agree. If you have only one form of income—the salary from your day job—you live in danger that something may happen to reduce or eliminate that income. If you lose your paycheck, you'll be left scrambling. In an unstable economy, layoffs, companies going out of business, early-retirement offers, and so on, are increasingly common. Too many people live paycheck to paycheck. However, wealthy people invest their money in a wide range of income-producing vehicles, including other businesses, real estate, tax shelters, and stocks and bonds that generate dividends. If one source of income dries up or disappears, they can still rely on the others. You should try to develop multiple streams of income, as well. You can do this by working part-time to accumulate savings, starting home-based or Web-based businesses, and by consulting a financial advisor to create a long-term investment strategy.

10. Invest for the Future

There are only two ways to make money legally in America: people at work and money at work. People at work make a living; money at work can make a fortune. *Money at work is why the rich get richer.*

Conventional wisdom insists that if you get a good education and work hard at your job, you'll get rich. In my observation, this is not true. With few exceptions, your job will not make you rich. It may allow you to live in a bigger house or drive a nicer car, but it will not make you rich. It may be fun and fulfilling, but it will not make you rich. What your job can do for you, however, is give you the initial capital you require to invest.

This is where you need to apply what you've learned about Motivational DNA to your finances. Are you driven by External Awards, such as money? Then use that motivation to envision what your life could be like ten years down the road if you sacrifice a little today by investing regularly and wisely. Are you motivated by Internal Awards? Then let your family, and the security you want to provide for them, become your impetus to invest.

Many people don't know how to start investing, so they become paralyzed and don't start at all. Unless you are motivated, it can be intimidating to begin. There seems to be an overwhelming

amount of information and an endless array of investment options to choose from. And each one carries a certain amount of
risk. I *know* how scary this can be—which is why every year we
train tens of thousands of people, from novices to veterans, how
to invest their money confidently, competently, *and conservatively*.
Everyone wants to make money, but we also need to be able to
sleep at night. If you don't know where or how to start, just go
online to www.FinancialSuccess.com, and our company will
assist you.

11.   Live Below Your Means

By living below your means, I do not mean that you should
suffer. Living below your means is about reducing nonessential
expenses and cutting costs in a way that doesn't make you feel
deprived of the things you need. It is a way to avoid unnecessary
debt. No matter what your Motivational DNA type, we all hate
the notion of our lives being dictated by the whim of a corpora-
tion or the erratic forces of the economy. Will you still have a job
tomorrow? Will you be able to pay the mortgage and buy gas in an
economic downturn? Living below your means is a way to give
you a measure of control and help you achieve financial freedom.

I recommend borrowing in only two circumstances: to fund
your education and to purchase a home. All the experts suggest
that your mortgage not exceed more than 28 percent of your
gross monthly income. If your house payment is too big, it can
leave you with too little money for other necessities, much less
such looming major expenses as retirement and college for your
children. I recommend that all your debt—including mortgage,
auto payments, and credit cards—be less than 37 percent of your
gross monthly earnings. If it's more than that, you need to find a
way to bring down your monthly debt obligation.

Drawing from the insights you've gained about your Motivational DNA, set up a plan to first reduce and then eliminate credit card debt. Avoid using credit cards for impulse and depreciating purchases. Start saving a portion of your pay through an automatic deduction program and sock away 10 percent or more of your pretax income each month. Gradually set aside money in an emergency fund so that you won't have to use credit cards when you need to replace a busted washing machine or repair a car.

Question every purchase. Do you really need to splurge on eating out again this week? When you do eat out, why not skip dessert and have it at home instead? When grocery shopping, buy store brands—they are usually indistinguishable from the more expensive brands. Buy used and save money on everything from books to boats. Utilize the Drives, Needs, and Awards that motivate you in order to live below your means and incorporate financial discipline into your life.

12. Improve Your Credit Score

A poor credit score will cost you money. Nearly all types of loans are approved or denied based on your credit score, which is provided to lenders by three national credit bureaus: Equifax, Experian, and TransUnion. The lower your score, the higher the interest rate you'll be charged and the more you'll pay in interest. Your credit score is also a determining factor in how much you'll be qualified to borrow for a home or a car.

You can improve your score by paying your bills on time and by reducing your overall debt load. Check your score with the three major reporting bureaus at least three to six months before seeking a mortgage or major loan so that you'll have time to raise your score before approaching lenders.

To improve your credit score, pay your bills on time, correct obvious mistakes on your credit report, reduce credit card balances, and pay off credit card debt rather than moving it to lower-rate cards. Your balance-to-credit-limit ratio—which is how much money you owe on your credit cards relative to your credit card limit—plays a significant part in determining your FICO score; try to keep your balances at or below 25 percent of your credit card limit. Since your balance-to-credit-limit ratio is crucial, moving balances to other credit cards and closing out the old accounts can hurt your FICO score. For example, if you have four credit cards, each with a $2,000 credit limit, your total credit limit would be $8,000. Say you owe a total of $2,000 on your four cards. Your total balance of $2,000 is 25 percent of your $8,000 credit limit. But if you transfer that $2,000 to two of the cards and cancel the other two, your total credit limit is reduced to $4,000 and your $2,000 balance accounts for 50 percent of the limit. This is likely to lower your credit score. Finally, don't open new credit card accounts, or close old ones, near the time you are going to apply for a loan.

13.   Strive to Achieve Great Results with Fewer Resources

The person who can do this will always be in demand. Don't throw money at every problem—throw creativity and brainpower at it instead.

14.   Embrace Lifelong Education

High achievers go out of their way to pursue educational opportunities. Motivated people are learners. And learners are earners. The investments you make in your own education can pay off handsomely, both financially and in your quality of life.

My friend Brian Tracy recently spoke at one of our GET MOTIVATED Seminars. Brian is an expert on corporate and personal performance, and he is the author of more than forty books. Here's what Brian had to say about lifelong education:

All skills are learnable. All business skills are learnable. All sales skills are learnable. All investment skills are learnable. And you can master all of these skills. You are so smart you could learn multiple languages. You can learn anything you need to learn to achieve any goal you have in life. Ask yourself, *What is the one skill that, if I mastered it, would improve my life the most?* Identify your weakest skill and work on it every day until you've mastered it. Make the rest of your life into a do-it-to-yourself project. In other words, your whole life becomes a series of taking your weakest skill and leapfrogging it forward. If you commit to strengthening your weakest and most needed skills—and if you do that for the rest of your life—I am convinced that you'll become one of the most competent, intelligent, sought-after, and highest-paid people in the country.

The Secret to Spiritual Fulfillment

Motivation and fulfillment go hand in hand—they are intricately intertwined. It's hard to remain motivated when you feel hollow or unsatisfied inside. While I haven't emphasized the power of spirituality in helping to ignite motivation, the fact remains that it is vital. You still need to utilize your Motivational DNA—the Drives and Needs and Awards that will help keep you energized, eager to take on new challenges and tackle more in life. But having a sense of purpose and a feeling of spiritual fulfillment is fundamental to fueling your motivation.

15. **Never Compromise Your Integrity**

    Always be honest and do what you know is right. Never compromise on your values or principles—they are what will sustain you in challenging times.

16.   **Know Who You Are and What You Believe**

Not all of us know what we believe in spiritually. And that's fine. There is no shame in not knowing what you believe spiritually. But there's no excuse for not seeking answers, for not being a seeker. Investigate spiritual truth. Become biblically literate. It was what I experienced when I read the Bible as a teenager that motivated me to completely turn my life around. Find out what you believe and why.

17.   **Live It**

If you don't live your beliefs, you don't really believe them. God-talk without virtuous action is hypocrisy. You've got to walk the talk.

18.   **Enjoy the Benefits of Community**

Studies show that you can have better health, live longer, make more money, enjoy more-satisfying relationships, and have higher self-esteem, a stronger marriage, and better relationships with your children through one simple decision—by attending the church of your faith regularly.

Worshipping with a community of like-minded people can produce significant physical, financial, and social advantages, as well as provide spiritual enrichment. People who attend worship services at least once a week tend to have a lower incidence of heart disease,[1] have lower blood pressure,[2] have better overall physical and mental health,[3] experience less depression,[4] are hospitalized less,[5] have lower mortality rates,[6] have less stress,[7] experience less substance abuse,[8] enjoy better social support, be less lonely,[9] live longer,[10] have more stable marriages,[11] and enjoy a higher level of income.[12] I consider that a phenomenal return on investment.

FREE BONUS #16
"Living a Life of Purpose" podcast by Tamara Lowe, plus
"Steps to Discovering Your Spiritual Purpose," a 15-page
Special Report ($79 value)

I know I'm breaking tradition, but I can't wait until the end of the chapter to give you your bonus! I am so excited about your next gift that I want to share it with you immediately. You were created on purpose, for a purpose, and then the real fun in life begins. Your last book bonus is a podcast I've recorded especially for you. It's called "Living a Life of Purpose." In it I share my personal spiritual journey and give you 5 ways to find, follow, and fulfill your course of destiny.

I'm also going to give you a special 15-page report on the remarkable benefits of spirituality, which includes a documented, summarized list of over 90 published medical reports citing double-blind studies done by world-renowned physicians and researchers. These studies highlight the amazing financial, social, and health benefits of spirituality. This is not a fuzzy, feel-good look at religion. On the contrary, there is a mountain of rock-solid scientific proof that reveals the evidence—if not the very existence—of a benevolent God.

Eight Ways to Win in Your Relationships

None of us can remain motivated all by ourselves. Even task-oriented Producers need strong connections with other people. So while the subject of relationships in a book on motivation may seem surprising, it's actually fundamental to inspiring great achievement. When we feel fulfilled in our personal relationships—with our family, friends, and those around us—we have more energy to take on professional challenges.

19.   Family First

No matter how much you accomplish, how many promotions you receive, or how much wealth you accumulate, if your relationship with your family suffers, it will diminish the joy of your other achievements. Life is too fleeting to spend it disconnected from your family. My definition of success is not measured in monetary terms. To me, success is when your adult children enjoy spending time with you. It's worth whatever sacrifices are necessary to strengthen your marriage, build friendship with your children, and improve your relationships with other family members.

20.   Inspire Others

Constantly seek to train, inspire, and encourage the people around you. You'll feel more motivated, and they will too. Strive to help others become better personally and professionally because of what they've learned from you.

21.   Treat Everyone with Respect

It's easy to respect those above you in the company hierarchy. However, you should be just as respectful of subordinates—and everyone else you come into contact with.

22.   When Someone Corrects You Regarding a Mistake You've Made (and We All Make Them), Be Grateful for the Correction

Don't just tolerate correction. Don't simply endure constructive criticism. Welcome it! Embrace it! Thank the other person for pointing out your mistake. Tell them, "I am 100 percent committed to change. I appreciate that you took the time to bring this to my attention. Anytime you see a way for me to improve, please don't hesitate to let me know."

When you screw up, do not defend yourself, justify your actions, or try to explain away your blunder. No one wants to hear an excuse. It just makes you look bad. Simply say, "I made a mistake and I am very, very sorry. This won't happen again. I will do whatever it takes to make it right." Take the blame—don't try to shift it. Shirking responsibility makes you appear irresponsible. Own your mistakes and strive to correct them.

23. Don't Complain

Winners are not whiners.

24. Keep Your Emotions in Check

Remain calm when others are irate. Never raise your voice in anger—no matter what the circumstance. Respond to provocation with grace and humility. Becoming visibly flustered demonstrates a lack of self-control.

25. Recall People's Names and the Details About Their Lives

You *can* remember people's names. Repeat their names when you first meet them. Use their names several times in your first conversation with them. This serves a twofold purpose: (1) people love to hear their names, and (2) it helps you engrave it in your memory.

There is no excuse for not remembering salient details about your colleagues, clients, and customers. Not remembering such details is just laziness. Make notes about people you meet shortly after you meet them. Note their hobbies, what is going on in their lives, their spouse's and children's names, and so on. Put it in your contacts list or address book. Ask about their family members by name the next time you see them. Inquire about their lives—their recent vacation, new home, or child's softball game. Expressing interest about their lives shows that you care about them personally as well as professionally.

26.   Remember, It's Not About You

Serve others. Don't be a prima donna. None of us are too good to do lowly jobs. Great leaders are happy to serve. They take on even menial tasks with enthusiasm.

The Five Pillars of Perfect Health

Motivation is enhanced by good health. When you don't feel well, it is difficult to maintain high motivation. Investing a small amount of effort to improve your health will increase your effectiveness, and your motivation, in every area of life.

27.   Energize with Exercise

Over the past year, my younger brother has lost seventy-five pounds. Brian was a chubby kid, a pudgy teen, and a stout young adult. Now in his late thirties, he has suddenly gotten himself into great condition, and he looks ten years younger.

"What motivated the change?" I asked him.

"I was scared of dying." Brian replied. "One night I was lying in bed and my heart was pounding wildly. I knew I was in terrible shape, and I was afraid to close my eyes because I wasn't sure I would wake up in the morning. That got my attention."

"That is scary," I said. "But how did you translate that into losing seventy-five pounds? What did you do?"

Brian said, "I thought about a friend of mine, the CEO of a huge company. This guy is in great shape. He runs marathons and competes in triathlons. He experiences the same pressures that I do in business, and I figured if he could make time for exercise, I could too. So I called him to get his advice.

"He told me that the only reason he is alive is because he runs.

He said he would not be able to manage his business—the demands are just too great—unless he worked out hard every day. He said running is the only thing that gets the stress off of him.

"That motivated me. I went out and bought a pair of running shoes that afternoon. I began by running one block. Then two blocks. Later, a mile. Now I can run eight miles without stopping. The weight melted off, and so did the stress. I'm in better shape now than I was when I was in high school. I feel fantastic. I exercise an hour a day and it's totally worth it. I wish I had started exercising twenty years ago!"

It is a medically substantiated fact that our health, brain function, and mood all improve when we exercise regularly. Try to work out five days a week. I know—you don't have time. Make the time. Start with a manageable program. Work with a personal coach if you need encouragement and support. Choose activities you enjoy. I don't like participating in team sports, but you might. Do what is fun for you. Yes, exercise is a commitment. Yes, it will cost you time and money. But diabetes and heart disease would cost you a lot more.

28. Get Enough Sleep

Blame it on the Internet, workplace stress, or *Late Night with Conan O'Brien,* but we are getting a lot less sleep than we should. Experts recommend seven and a half to eight hours. But too many people sleep an average of just six hours each night.

This has a detrimental impact on motivation. It can affect our ability to learn and our memory, weight, stamina, health, and safety. Above all else, it affects our disposition.

Refrain from heavy meals, caffeine, and vigorous exercise near bedtime. Close the computer. Put away the PDA. Shut down your cell phone. Turn off the TV and go to bed earlier.

29. Eat Responsibly

You've heard the old adage "You are what you eat" a thousand times, but it's true. Make quality decisions about what you eat and drink. If you are overweight, lose the weight; you'll feel healthier and have more energy. And people will notice the difference in the way you look.

There are addictive properties to certain foods and drinks. Identify those items and cut them out of your diet. I love sweets. But I rarely eat them. Why? I'm a former drug addict. I know all about addictive behavior. For me, succumbing to a little dessert could easily lead to cake and cookies and chocolate after every meal.

Can't help finishing off that pint of Ben & Jerry's ice cream? Then don't buy it in the first place. If it's not in the house, you can't fall prey to temptation in the middle of the night. Did you know that if you simply eliminated two teaspoons of sugar from your coffee each morning, and did nothing else differently, you'd lose twenty-two pounds in one year? Small, painless changes can be the secret to easy weight loss.

A few years ago, I had dinner with a famous television personality. When she was finished with her meal, my friend unscrewed the saltshaker and liberally doused salt on her leftovers. Seeing the look of surprise on my face, she said, "Now I'm not tempted to eat those last few bites." Hey, whatever works. Little tricks like that can be the key to keeping the pounds from creeping on.

Try calorie bargains. Swap a high-calorie food for something lower-calorie that you like just as much. It's not about deprivation—it's about equal pleasure with less consequence. For instance, two premium dark chocolate truffles are 200 calories. A bargain? It could be—if it's in place of the 600-calorie cheesecake you were going to eat. Here is an example of how I might use calorie bargains at lunch:

- Unlimited sparkling water with lime (0 calories) instead of a small glass of orange juice (150 calories)
- Cucumber with garlic salt (40 calories) instead of tortilla chips (200 calories)
- Clementine (35 calories) instead of an apple (100 calories)

That's 375 less calories—just at lunch! This kind of calorie deficit on a daily basis would result in thirty-nine pounds of weight loss in one year.

Remember, food is fuel. You wouldn't dump a milk shake into your gas tank—it would ruin your car. Your body is far more valuable than your automobile, so make conscientious choices about how you care for it.

30. Get Regular Physical Checkups

Annual exams can help spot medical conditions before symptoms appear. Fortunately, the majority of diseases can be treated if caught early enough. Have a complete physical exam along with at least one dental visit every year. Be sure that you receive all the recommended tests and procedures for your age and gender.

31. Make Time for Rest and Relaxation

Taking annual vacations and periodic weekend getaways will lower your stress level, improve your health, and let you enjoy life more. Forty-six percent of U.S. employees feel overworked. Twenty-five percent of Americans don't even take the vacation they're entitled to. This can ultimately have a negative impact on job performance, employee retention, workplace safety, and health care. Enjoy periods of rest, reflection, and relaxation with the people you love. You deserve it—we all do. It's good for your health, your career, and your family.

Follow these rules and I'm confident that your motivation and energy will soar. You will be able to better utilize your Motivational DNA for success in everything you do.

Finish First and Finish Well

Bobby Fischer was the greatest chess player in the history of the game. Inside the sixty-four squares on the chess board, Fischer was a genius. A child prodigy and grand master by the age of fifteen, he won the U.S. Chess Championship all eight times that he competed. He was the first, and so far the only, American to win the official World Chess Championship.

Although he was a brilliant chess master, Fischer was eccentric and egotistical. His talent was tarnished by his arrogance. Not even his fans were exempt from his contempt. Following a tournament win in Argentina, an admirer called out, "Great game, Bobby." Fischer barked back, "How would *you* know?"

Fischer was stripped of his world champion title for refusing to defend it and spent the last three decades of his life as a recluse. When he occasionally surfaced, he would utter vile, anti-Semitic remarks, despite the fact that his own mother was Jewish. Hours after the terrorist attacks on September 11, 2001, Fischer, in a radio interview, said, "This is all wonderful news. I applaud the act. I want to see the U.S. wiped out." Fischer may have finished first in chess, but he didn't finish well in life. When he died in 2008, the *Wall Street Journal* called him "an embarrassment to be apologized for, belittled or ignored."

To finish first is thrilling. But there's something even better than finishing first. It's called *finishing well*. In golf, players strive for a full swing with complete follow-through. Pro golfers say, "You have to finish well to play well." In life, it's the other way around. *You have to play well to finish well.*

Let me ask you a question. What do you think of when you hear the name O. J. Simpson? How about Michael Vick? Pete Rose? Darryl Strawberry? Mike Tyson? The first thing that comes to mind is probably not their extraordinary athletic abilities, but rather their subpar behavior. Finishing first is important, but finishing well is imperative. A person may start off with a bang and accomplish great things, but it doesn't mean that he or she will finish well.

Celebrity stupidity dominates the headlines these days—from DUIs to profane tirades to repeated rounds of rehab—but neither Hollywood nor professional sports has a monopoly on misconduct. Improprieties occur in business, politics, and every sector of society. There are any number of ways to crash and burn.

The athletes I mentioned above are gifted individuals, and I admire their athletic achievements. My intent is not to name and shame them. I'm a former drug addict, dealer, and dropout. I was the poster child for bad behavior. Who am I to judge? My heart breaks for these people. And I'm not writing any of them off. I know firsthand that redemption is possible—even from the deepest, darkest places. The good news is that the score doesn't count at halftime! There's still a lot of game left to play; the final score has not yet been posted. It's how we finish that matters.

Here's My Point: Your Character Will Always Eclipse Your Talent

No matter how gifted you are, you can't hide behind your gifts. Who you are is far more valuable than what you do. Consider the examples of people like Margaret Thatcher, Ronald Reagan, Mother Teresa, and others that I've highlighted in this book. I implore you to be wise. Be kind. Do right. Starting strong is important; sustaining the action is crucial. But how we finish becomes our legacy. So use your Motivational DNA to advance in your career, achieve your goals, inspire others, and, above all else . . . finish well.

APPENDIX A:
GOAL ACHIEVEMENT BLUEPRINT

The Goal: _____

The Deadline: _____

With your goal in mind, answer the questions below for *each of your three primary motivational factors*. Include as much detail as possible for each of your answers.

Connectors

➤ What organizations can I connect with to help me achieve my goal?

_____
_____
_____

➤ Who has successfully accomplished the same (or a similar) goal and can help me strategize to overcome the obstacles I will encounter?

_____

_____

_____

➤ What groups can I join to support me and fuel my motivation?

_____

_____

_____

➤ Who can encourage me to stay on track and help make me accountable?

_____

_____

_____

Producers

➤ How can I turn this goal into a competition?

_____

_____

_____

➤ What obstacles and distractions will I need to navigate in order to achieve my goal?

_____

_____

_____

➤ How will I overcome those obstacles?

_____

_____

_____

➤ Which people, groups, and organizations can I deploy to help me do the heavy lifting?

_____

_____

_____

Stabilizers

➤ What existing systems and structures can I utilize to help me reach my goal?

_____

_____

_____

➤ What can I do now to research and create a methodology that will help me succeed?

_____

_____

_____

➤ How can I eliminate distractions and focus on doing something every day that will cause me to make progress toward accomplishing my goal?

_____

_____

_____

➤ How will achieving my goal add balance and stability to my life?

_____

_____

_____

Variables

➤ What can I do to add fun to the equation and at the same time advance me toward my goal?

_____

_____

_____

➤ What are the most creative and interesting ways to accomplish my goal?

_____

_____

_____

➤ If Plan A doesn't work, what will I do for Plans B through Z?

_____

_____

_____

➤ How will I add variety, joy, and excitement to the process so that I don't get bored?

_____

_____

_____

Internals

➤ Why is this goal meaningful to me?

_____

_____

_____

➤ How will it make a positive difference to others?

_____

_____

_____

➤ What are the things that will keep me from quitting when the going gets tough or the pace becomes tedious?

_____

_____

_____

➤ What inner resources will I utilize to take action daily toward my goal?

_____

_____

_____

Externals

➤ How will I personally benefit by achieving this goal?

_____

_____

_____

➤ What incremental rewards can I build into the process to help me accomplish my goal?

_____

_____

_____

➤ How does realizing this goal set me up for even greater success?

_____

_____

_____

➤ What big reward will I give myself when I cross the finish line?

_____

_____

_____

APPENDIX B:
TOP TEN LIFETIME GOALS

What are the top ten things that you really want out of life?

Writing down your goals forces you to visualize them. It also creates emotional commitment. Be sure to include a deadline and the steps you will take to achieve your goals. If you set your goal for the *cause,* the effect will take care of itself. For example, rather than writing, "I want to learn Italian," it is better to write, "I am learning to speak Italian by signing up for a night class and studying ten minutes a day until I am fluent."

1. _____

_____

_____

2. _____
_____
_____

3. _____
_____
_____

4. _____
_____
_____

5. _____
_____
_____

6. _____
_____
_____

7. _____
_____
_____

8. _____
_____
_____

9. _____
_____
_____

10. _____
_____
_____

APPENDIX C:
TAMARA LOWE'S
CHARITY PARTNERS

AmeriCares: AmeriCares is a nonprofit international relief organization that delivers medicines, medical supplies, and aid to children and adults in crisis across America and around the world. We've delivered more than $8 billion in humanitarian aid to 137 countries. When disasters strike, it's natural to wish you could help. With AmeriCares, you can. Visit www.AmeriCares.org or call (800) 486-HELP to get involved.

Big Brothers Big Sisters: Big Brothers Big Sisters helps vulnerable children overcome negative odds. Our service has proven to reduce children's risk of skipping school, behaving violently, using drugs and alcohol, and falling victim to other negative cycles. With nearly 400 agencies across the country, Big Brothers Big Sisters serves more than a quarter million children. Learn how you can join the movement to change how children grow up in America by going to www.BigBrothersBigSisters.org.

Boys To Men: Boys To Men is a nonprofit organization that counsels young men between the ages of 13–17 who struggle with low self-esteem, dishonesty, lack of motivation and direction, anger management, defiance and disrespect, academic under-achievement, drug abuse, self-destructive behavior and criminal activities. The organization aims to prepare young men to be responsible, productive individuals in society by emphasizing the importance of education and work ethic. To get involved please call (340) 692-7737.

Children International: Children International's programs benefit over 300,000 poor children and their families in 11 countries around the world, including Chile, Colombia, the Dominican Republic, Ecuador, Guatemala, Honduras, India, Mexico, the Philippines, Zambia, and the United States. Established in 1936, Children International is a nonprofit organization with its headquarters in Kansas City, Missouri. To sponsor a child living in poverty, visit www.children.org today.

Children's Memorial Hospital (Chicago): Children's Memorial is recognized as one of the top pediatric hospitals in the country and is dedicated to the health and well-being of *all* children. We have a 125-year history of providing compassionate care in a family-centered environment, staffing top pediatric specialists, using the latest technologies, and offering valuable kid-focused experience. To learn more or make a donation, please contact Children's Memorial Foundation at (773) 880-4237 or visit www.childrensmemorial.org.

Children's Miracle Network: Children's Miracle Network is an international nonprofit organization that raises funds for more than 170 children's hospitals. Over 90 organizations, 400 media partners, and countless individuals unite with Children's Miracle Network hospitals to help sick and injured kids in local communities. Donations to Children's Miracle Network create miracles by funding medical care, research, and education that save and improve the lives of 17 million children each year. To learn more visit www.childrensmiraclenetwork.org.

Christopher & Dana Reeve Foundation: Dedicated to curing spinal cord injuries by funding innovative research and improving the quality of life for people living with paralysis, The Reeve Foundation makes grants to outstanding organizations that help those living with paralysis and their caregivers. We have helped tens of thousands of children and adults living with paralysis, and their families, with useful, often life-saving and life-changing information. For more information, please visit our website at www.ChristopherReeve.org or call 800-225-0292.

Compassion International: In response to the Great Commission, Compassion International exists as an advocate for children, to release them from their spiritual, economic, social, and physical poverty and enable them to become responsible and fulfilled Christian adults. We provide child development programs and speak out for children in poverty. Compassion International helps more than 1 million children in 24 countries. To find out more about Compassion International, please visit us at www.compassion.com or call us at (800) 336-7676.

East Gates: East Gates International is a nonprofit organization dedicated to supporting and facilitating a growing, positive relationship between the U.S. and China. One of East Gates' main areas of focus is to provide greatly needed assistance to mentally and physically challenged children. East Gates also provides materials for churches and school libraries and grants educational scholarships for youth from impoverished areas. Tamara Lowe serves on the Board of Directors for East Gates, which is led by Ned Graham, the youngest son of Billy and Ruth Graham. For more information please visit www.eastgates.org.

Feed the Children: Feed the Children is consistently ranked as one of the 10 largest international charities in the U.S., based on private, non-governmental support. We deliver food, medicine, clothing and other necessities to individuals, children, and families who lack these essentials due to famine, war, poverty, or natural disasters. In 2007, Feed the Children

distributed more than 135 million pounds of food and other essentials to children and their families in all 50 states and in 32 countries. Since its founding, we have helped people in need in 118 countries around the globe. For more information, please visit www.feedthechildren.org.

Feed the Hungry: There's really no excuse for a child to go hungry. Since 1987, Feed the Hungry has brought help and hope to children in over 90 nations of the world. Through the Every Child Every Day initiative thousands of children in Africa, Asia, and Central America come to schools and care centers knowing that someone loves them enough to provide their "daily bread." Find out how you can bring real change to the lives of vulnerable children for pennies a day, please contact www.feedthehungry.org or call 866-223-4583.

Global Teen Challenge: Teen Challenge is a nonprofit organization that works with teens and families, providing drug prevention training and offering recovery programs for those who are addicted to drugs and affected by other life-controlling problems. With a 50-year history, Teen Challenge is one of the world's largest privately funded organizations dealing with substance abuse. Find out how to volunteer in the 200 Teen Challenge centers in the U.S., as well as 800 centers internationally, or provide scholarships for teens in need at www.TeenChallengeUSA.com.

Heath Evans Foundation: The Heath Evans Foundation is dedicated to fostering hope and healing in the lives of children and families affected by sexual abuse. We are committed to breaking the cycle of abuse through healing the psychological, physical, and spiritual wounds inflicted on innocent children, and bringing hope and healing to the young victims of sexual abuse. The Heath Evans Foundation works in at-risk communities and provides access to a variety of programs, treatments, and services in communities with great need and scarce resources. To get involved please call (561) 282-6345 or visit our website at www.heathevans.org.

Jesus Loves You Ministries: Jesus Loves You Ministries provides food, clothing, medical supplies, counseling and the love of Christ to young people who congregate at Rainbow Gatherings that are held around the world. You can read more about our outreach to today's trouble youth in chapter 9 of *Get Motivated!* Find out more about us and our outreaches on our website at www.KingdomPromotions.org or call 785-632-3357.

Jewish Children's Regional Service: At 153 years old, we are the oldest Jewish children's agency in the U.S., as well as the only regional Jewish children's agency in the country. Our social service agency and charitable fund supports low-income and dependent Jewish youth who live across a wide expanse of the southern United States. Many of those funded live in single-parent households, or are being reared by family members other than their parents. Learn how you can get involved by visiting us online at www.jcrsnola.org.

Joshua House (Tampa Bay, FL): Eighteen years ago, a group of concerned citizens dreamed of a safe haven for the abused, neglected and abandoned children in the Tampa Bay area. That dream was realized in the creation of Joshua House, a nonprofit, therapeutic residential shelter that provides a safe, nurturing, family-like environment for children 12 and younger. These children have been removed from their homes by the Department of Children and Families and have been through multiple foster homes due to significant abuse. To get involved, please contact us at www.friendsofjoshuahouse.com or call 813-263-3469.

Joshua House (Tyrone, PA): Joshua House is incorporated as a nonprofit, charitable organization that provides a safe place where young people can come to recreate and receive counseling and life skills training. Founded by Jim Kilmartin, the Mayor of Tyrone, Pennsylvania, Joshua House is making a positive impact in the lives of today's youth. To find out how you can volunteer or contribute, please visit us online at www.joshuahousetyrone.org or call 814-937-7395.

Kids Charity of Tampa Bay, Inc.: Dedicated to improving the quality of life for foster children and foster families, Kids Charity of Tampa Bay assists abused, neglected, or abandoned children by raising funds and developing resources. Funds raised by Kids Charity of Tampa Bay will go toward building a 48-bed emergency assessment shelter, providing emergency financial support to foster families and children in crisis, and supporting child service programs. Please contact us at (813) 263-3469 to find out how you can help.

Luis Palau Association: Youth around the world are searching for hope and truth. And the Luis Palau Association is answering. Today, through LPA's two-day outdoor festivals, area-wide community service projects, Livin It® action sports, Next Generation Alliance®, and a variety of media (books, radio, Internet resources, etc.), hundreds of thousands of youth are learning how they can make a difference in their own communities. Find out how you can get involved today by visiting www.palau.org or calling (503) 614-1500.

MAZON: A Jewish Response to Hunger: MAZON ("food" in Hebrew) is a leader in the global anti-hunger movement. As the only national Jewish organization whose sole focus is hunger relief, we help to provide nourishment and promote self-sufficiency for hundreds of thousands of people at risk of hunger in America, in Israel, and around the world. Since 1985, MAZON has granted nearly $50 million to emergency food providers, food banks, multi-service organizations, and advocacy groups that seek solutions to the problem of hunger. To learn more please visit www.mazon.org or call (310) 442-0020.

Mercy Corps: Since 1979, Mercy Corps has provided more than $1.5 billion in assistance to people in 106 nations. We work in the midst of disasters, conflicts, chronic poverty, and instability to help people win against nearly impossible odds. Over the past five years, more than 89 percent of the agency's resources have been allocated directly to programs that help people in need. For more information on how to donate or be involved, visit www.mercycorps.org.

National Alliance to End Homelessness: The National Alliance to End Homelessness is a nonpartisan organization committed to preventing and ending homelessness in the United States. We work collaboratively with the public, private, and nonprofit sectors to build state and local capacity, leading to stronger programs and policies that help communities achieve their goal of ending homelessness. To learn more about the Alliance or to contribute to our work, visit www.endhomelessness.org.

National House of Hope: Founded in 2001 by former schoolteacher Sara Trollinger, House of Hope is a residential program for healing America's teens and reconciling families. Presently, there are well over 50 Houses of Hope in process across the country. National House of Hope and HOH Orlando, as well as other HOH affiliates, receive no government funds, depending solely on the private sector for funding. To donate or to receive more information, please contact www.nationalhouseofhope.org or call (407) 422-6135.

Operation Smile: Operation Smile is a worldwide children's medical charity whose network of global volunteers are dedicated to helping improve the health and lives of children and young adults. Since its founding in 1982, Operation Smile volunteers have treated more than 120,000 children born with cleft lips, cleft palates, and other facial deformities, and the organization has a presence in 51 countries. In addition to contributing free medical treatment, Operation Smile trains local medical professionals in its partner countries and leaves behind crucial equipment to lay the groundwork for long-term self-sufficiency. For more information, visit www.operationsmile.org.

Place of Hope: Place of Hope is a state-licensed child welfare organization providing family-style foster care (emergency and long-term); family outreach and intervention; transitional housing and support services; adoption and foster care recruitment and support; hope and healing opportunities for children and families who have been traumatized by abuse and neglect. To learn how to get involved, visit our websites www.placeofhope.com and www.villagesofhope.net.

Project HOPE: Since 1958, Project HOPE has fulfilled a promise of Health Opportunities for People Everywhere. By educating health professionals and community health workers, providing medicines and supplies, strengthening health facilities, and fighting diseases such as TB, HIV/AIDS, and diabetes, Project HOPE has improved health and saved lives in more than 100 countries. To support and participate in Project HOPE's work, please visit www.projecthope.org.

Project Rescue International: Project Rescue supports transformational aftercare for survivors of sexual slavery and trafficking, as well as raising awareness and mobilizing others to challenge the injustice of sex trafficking worldwide. Project Rescue provides hope, freedom, and the opportunity for new life for survivors of sexual slavery and children at risk.

For more information, please contact Project Rescue International at www.projectrescueintl@sbcglobal.net.

Seattle Children's Hospital: Seattle Children's delivers superior patient care, advances new discoveries and treatments through pediatric research, and serves as the pediatric and adolescent academic medical referral center for the largest landmass of any children's hospital in the country (Washington, Alaska, Montana, and Idaho). We are internationally recognized for advancing discoveries in cancer, genetics, immunology, pathology, infectious disease, injury prevention, and bioethics. For more information, visit www.seattlechildrens.org.

Sister to Sister: Sister to Sister is a nonprofit organization that teaches girls between the ages of 13–17 moral responsibility, how to interact with their peers and the richness of building family relationships. Sister to Sister seeks to build self-esteem and self-worth and emphasizes the value of education, preparing young women for college and post-secondary studies. To find out how you can help, please call us at (340) 778-1575.

Teen Mania: Teen Mania offers high-impact youth events, life-changing mission trips, resources for youth ministries and families, and internship opportunities in ministry, media, or music. Tamara Lowe's husband, Peter, has served on the Board of Directors for Teen Mania and is a strong supporter of their work. Learn about how you can get involved or contribute at www.teenmania.com.

The Dream Center: The Dream Center is a non-profit outreach dedicated to helping children, families, and individuals in the inner-cities. We provide food, clothing, shelter, life rehabilitation, education and job training, love, and much more through our 273 outreaches. We reach thousands of hurting and needy children, families and adults each week. Find out more information about how you can help at www.dreamcenter.org or call (213) 273-7000.

The King's Academy: Established in 1970, The King's Academy serves more than 1,250 students from preschool through 12th grade. Each year, The King's Academy returns a portion of its tuition to families in need in the form of scholarships and financial assistance. TKA students contribute more than 20,000 hours of community service per year by volunteering in programs and projects that positively impact those who are hurting and in need. For more information about The King's Academy, visit www.TKA.net.

Toys for Tots: Toys for Tots is a charitable program run by the U.S. Marine Corps Reserve. We provide happiness and hope to disadvantaged children who might otherwise be overlooked during the Christmas holiday season. Our gifts offer these children recognition, confidence, and a positive memory that will last them for a lifetime. It is such experiences that help motivate them to become responsible and caring members of their community. The Marine Corps fulfilled the holiday hopes of 7.5 million needy children in 2007, but sadly we still ran out of toys long before we ran out of children. To get involved please visit www.toysfortots.org or call (703) 640-9433.

Urban Youth Impact: Founder & President Bill Hobbs left his professional golf career in 1988 to work with at-risk youth. In 1997, he started Urban Youth Impact, a faith-based nonprofit organization that helps inner-city youth and their families. UYI's community programs and annual events touch 250 kids every week and 5,000 families every year. The 32,000-square-foot Dream Center, purchased in 2005, is UYI's outreach facility that houses the largest free clinic in Palm Beach County, and, after renovations are complete, a youth center. To help us change lives, contact us at www.urbanyouthimpact.com or 561-832-9220.

Youth with a Mission: YWAM is an international faith-based movement of mostly young volunteers from many different backgrounds and denominations. They have united in their desire to help make a difference in a needy world. YWAM's activities span the globe and YWAM's 15,000 volunteer staff are active in about 1,000 locations in 170 countries. Financial support can be directed through "YWAM Support" online at www.ywam.org.

World Vision: World Vision is a Christian humanitarian organization dedicated to working with children, families, and their communities worldwide by tackling the causes of poverty and injustice. Motivated by our faith in Jesus Christ, World Vision serves alongside the poor and oppressed in more than 100 countries as a demonstration of God's unconditional love for all people. You can join us and help bring clean water, medical care, education, food, microfinance loans and emergency relief to those who need it most by visiting www.worldvision.org.

For a complete listing of Tamara Lowe's charity partners, and to find out how you can help needy children around the world, please visit www.GetMotivatedBook.com.

ENDNOTES

1. When I began my research, I had no idea that it would result in my writing a book about motivational typology. I had questions about motivation and was searching for answers, primarily to satisfy my own curiosity. I am blessed with access to a lot of free data because of the large audiences that we conduct seminars for. Since I am responsible for preparing attendee survey forms, I began to add questions to the surveys about motivation. The more questions I asked, the more questions I had. Soon the data exceeded my ability to analyze it by hand. I recruited my data entry and IT departments to input the information and run reports for me. With the help of my team, I was able to process and segment the information by gender, age, income, profession, and numerous other criterion. What we now know as Motivational DNA began to emerge. Michelangelo said, "Every block of marble has a statue inside." As we chiseled, the statue emerged.

CHAPTER 3

1. Steve Beller, Ph.D., "Workplace Wellness Programs: Motivating Employees to Live Healthy," *Wall Street Journal,* January 26, 2008.
2. Lars-Eric Olsson, Doctoral Theses from Sahlgrenska Academy, 2006.
3. Birgitta E. M. Grahn, Lars A. Borgquist, and Charlotte S. Ekdahl, "Motivated Patients Are More Cost Effectively Rehabilitated," Cambridge University Press, May 25, 2001.

CHAPTER 4

1. Buckingham & Coffman, 1999.
2. Naish & Birdi, 2001.
3. Dean R. Spritzer, *Super-Motivation,* AMACOM, 1995.
4. "Gallup Study: Engaged Employees Inspire Company Innovation," *Gallup Management Journal,* October 12, 2006.
5. J. Krueger and E. Killham. At work feeling good matters; happy employees are better equipped to handle workplace relationships, stress and change according to the latest GMJ survey [Electronic version], *Gallup Management Journal,* 2005. Available from http://www.gallup.com/.

CHAPTER 10

1. "Workplace Index" (Towers Perrin, 1997). National survey of 2,500 employees' attitudes about work and pay.
2. Carla O'Dell and Jerry McAdams, "People, Performance, and Pay," American Productivity Center and the American Compensation Association, 1987. A survey of 1,598 members of the American Productivity Center and of the American Compensation Association.
3. WorldatWork and Sibson & Company, 2000, "The Rewards of Work—What Employees Value." A survey of over 1,200 randomly selected U.S. employees determining the value of financial and nonfinancial rewards on attraction, retention, and motivation by employment size, employee age, and industry.
4. The Consortium for Alternative Rewards Strategies Research, "Organizational Performance & Rewards: 663 Experiences in Making the Link," 1994. Reviewed effectiveness of variable pay plans in 663 companies over a three-year period.

CHAPTER 16

1. U. Goldbourt, S. Yaari, and J. H. Mealie. "Factors predictive of long-term coronary heart disease mortality among 10,059 male Israeli civil servants and municipal employees," *Cardiology* 82 (2–3):100–21, 1993; J.D. Kark, G. Shemi, Y. Friedlander, et al., 1996. "Does religious observance promote health?: Mortality in secular vs. Religious kibbutzim in Israel," *American Journal of Public Health* 86(3):341–46.

2. J. S. Levin and H. Y. Vanderpool. "Is religion therapeutically significant for hypertension?" *Soc Sci Med* 29(1):69–78, 1989; D. B. Larson, H. G. Koenig, B. H. Kaplan, et al., 1989; "The impact of religion on men's blood pressure," *Journal of Religion and Health,* 28:265–78, 1989.

3. B. G. Frankel and W. E. Hewitt. "Religion and well-being among Canadian university students: the role of faith groups on campus," *Journal for the Scientific Study of Religion* 33(1):62–73, 1994.

4. H. G. Koenig, J. C. Hays, L. K. George, D. G. Blazer, D. B. Larson, L. R. Landerman, "Modeling the cross-sectional relationships between religion, physical health, social support and depressive symptoms," *Am J Geriatr Psychiatry* 5(2):131–44, 1997.

5. Michele Lesie, "Studies find validity in faith's healing power/Religion good for health, scientists say." Data cited from a Duke University study published in the *Southern Medical Journal," Minneapolis Star Tribune,* November 28, 1998.

6. J. S. House, C. Robbins and H. L. Metzner, "The association of social relationships and activities with mortality: Prospective evidence from the Tecumseh Community Health Study," *American Journal of Epidemiology,* 116:(1)123–40, 1982; L. F. Berkman and S. L. Syme, "Social networks, host resistance, and morality: A nine-year follow-up study of Alameda County residents," *American Journal of Epidemiology* 109(2):186–204, 1979; T. E. Seeman, G.A. Kaplan, L. Knudsen, et al., "Social ties and mortality in Evans County, Georgia," *American Journal of Epidemiology* 123(4):714–23, 1987; W. J. Strawbridge, R. D. Cohen, S. J. Shema, et al., "Frequent attendance at religious services and mortality over 28 years," *American Journal of Public Health* 87(6):957–61, June 19, 1997; V. J. Schoenbach, B. H., Kaplan, L. Fredman, et al., "Social network ties and mortality in Evans County, Georgia," *Ameican Journal of Epidemiology* 126(4):577–91, 1986; S. Bryant and W. Rakowski, "Predictors of mortality among elderly African-Americans." *Research on Aging* 14(1):50–67, 1992.

7. *Minneapolis Star Tribune,* ibid.

8. K. A. Khavari and T. M. Harmon, "The relationship between degree of professed religious belief and use of drugs," *International Journal of Addictions* 17(5):847–57, 1982.

9. H. G. Koenig, J. C. Hays, L. K.George, D. G. Blazer, D. B. Larson., and L.R. Landerman, "Modeling the cross-sectional relationships between religion, physical health, social support and depressive symptoms," *Am J Geriatr Psychiatry* 5(2):131–44, 1997.

10. W. J. Strawbridge, R. D. Cohen, S. J. Shema, and G. A. Kaplan, "Frequent attendance at religious services and mortality over 28 years," *Am J Public Health* 87(6):957–61, 1997.

11. D. Larson, M. G. Milano, and C. Barry, "Religion: the forgotten factor in health care." *The World & I,* February 1, 1996.

12. Maggie Gallagher, "Religion Is Good for Your Health," *Dallas Morning News,* February 12, 1996, page 15A.

INDEX